A B
Busine
& Property Insurance in the UK

CW00493714

How to get the best deal and the right cover

NIGEL ADAMS

WORDCATCHERpublishing

A Buyer's Guide to Business, Commercial, and Property Insurance
How to get the best deal and the right cover

© 2020 Nigel Adams
Source images supplied by Adobe Stock
Cover design © David Norrington

The Author asserts the moral right to be identified as the author of this work. All rights reserved. This book is protected under the copyright laws of the United Kingdom. Any reproduction or other unauthorised use of the material or artwork herein is prohibited without the express written permission of the Publisher.

No part of this book may be reproduced, stored in a retrieval system, or transmitted in any form or by any means, electronic, electrostatic, magnetic tape, mechanical, photocopying, recording or otherwise, without the written permission of the Publisher.

British Library Cataloguing in Publication Data.
A catalogue record for this book is available from the British Library.

Published in the United Kingdom by Wordcatcher Publishing Group Ltd
www.wordcatcher.com
Tel: 02921 888321
Facebook.com/WordcatcherPublishing

First Edition: 2020

Print edition ISBN: 9781789421019
Ebook edition ISBN: 9781789421477

Category: Business / Insurance

CONTENTS

ACKNOWLEDGEMENTS

I would like to dedicate this book to some very special people.

My father, Peter Adams, who lived a life of honour and adventure. First serving in the Royal Air Force as a pilot in WWII, then returned to live a considerate life as a professional in the financial services sector. Dad taught me it is more important to give people a service and care about what you do, than how much money you make.

My mother, Nadine, who met and married my father in Cardiff in 1961. She was always a loving, strong mother and a supportive wife. My sister and I had lots of fun as kids and had a great childhood. We even had a pony. Mum worked with Dad in the family business until Dad died in 1997. They were a team I admired and respected.

My wife, Karen, has been my rock. Always by my side, unfailingly loving and selfless, Karen has given me complete support and encouragement in everything I have done. She has believed in me when that was all I had. She is the love of my life, the reason I get up every morning and keep going. She is the mother to one of my daughters and her vision keeps me going when I am flagging. I hope I fulfil all her hopes and dreams.

Finally, I would like to thank my daughters; Fiona, Jennifer and Ellie. They have taught me that there is magic in this world, and that good things come to those who get up every day and work hard. They are strong young women, clever, kind, intelligent and considerate. I am deeply proud of them. I know they will be the best they can be, long after I am gone. I hope my memory and my example helps them get on in life.

INTRODUCTION

This book is for business people interested in finding the best deal for their business, commercial or property insurance in the United Kingdom. It is focused on commercial rather than personal insurance, as greater complexity exists here. I have included a small section relating to personal insurances, as businessmen and women still need to satisfy their own personal requirements.

Over nearly four decades, I have repeatedly found that individuals exercising this responsibility often make poor decisions because they don't understand the market or how it operates. This means they end up unknowingly paying higher premiums, even when they think they have a good deal, or they are less well-protected than they should be, and over-exposed to risk.

My aim is to provide clear and concise information in a no-nonsense way so customers can make intelligent decisions and get the best deal. Best does not always equate to cheapest though. You can pay less for a premium, only to find when you need it, it doesn't cover your losses. Getting the right solution means matching a competitive price with the widest and most appropriate cover, from a well-known and respected insurer, who will remain sympathetic when a claim arises.

My earnest passion is to see that customers make intelligent decisions when purchasing insurance. Whilst it is seldom something customers think about very much outside of their renewal window, if understood correctly, the purchase can literally save a business. This flows through to protecting jobs and livelihood of their families. Surely, no one would prefer to be on income support, and no director, principal or partner would rather contemplate liquidation or redundancies just because they did not understand the insurance purchase.

As an experienced broker, I have seen almost everything under the sun and dealt with a vast range of individuals, businesses and the claims that flow from events beyond their control. Claims are of great concern and it is at this point the correct insurance cover can deliver peace of mind and reassurance. When insurance is understood and purchased intelligently, not only is the correct cover obtained but in most cases it saves money.

If, however, your only concern is getting the cheapest price every year, then I earnestly suggest you put this book back on the shelf and continue to use your own judgement. I guarantee that a time will come when you need professional advice, and the support you get will be far more important than the price you paid.

Nigel Adams TD VR Dip. CII
Managing Director
Severn Bay Corporate Solutions Limited

DISCLAIMER

If you read and apply the information in this book, you will achieve a competitive price for your insurance with adequate cover for your situation. However, the author cannot guarantee the result you ultimately negotiate with brokers or insurers. This can only be achieved by a customer carrying out a detailed fact-find with an experienced, professional broker and engaging in an open market search to find the best product.

I am open to discussing the individual needs of customers should they wish to engage with me. Enquiries can be made to Severn Bay via our website, www.severnbay.com, where you can also see what our customers say and use the contact form or call us for a chat.

GLOSSARY

The insurance industry uses many technical terms, usually to define precise meaning. These terms are not always understandable for the inexperienced. This section clarifies meanings of keywords and phrases you'll find in insurance documents, and within this book and is based upon definitions from the British Insurance Brokers Association with their agreement. If you are unsure about any of these terms seek professional advice.

ACCIDENTAL DAMAGE

Any damage to things, such as dropping a vase, or glass shattering when a door slams, other than those things already covered like Storm, Flood, Fire as specified perils.

ACT OF GOD (VIS MAJOR)

"Natural causes directly and exclusively, without human intervention and that could not have been prevented by any amount of foresight and pains and care reasonably to have been expected." Nugent v Smith (1876). Things that happen which are completely out of the blue and did not involve an active agent.

ADDENDUM

A document setting out agreed alterations to an insurance contract. (See also ENDORSEMENT).

ADDITIONAL PREMIUM

A further premium payable by the insured as a result of policy amendment that may have increased the risk or changed the policy conditions or sum insured. For example, the addition of a new driver on a motor policy after it has been issued. A further payment due because of a change to the terms. For example, adding a new driver on a motor policy after it has been issued.

ADJUSTER

One who investigates and assesses claims on behalf of insurers (also known as a claims adjuster or a loss adjuster).

ADVANCE PROFITS INSURANCE

Insurance of the expected profits of a new enterprise, or of an extension to an existing business, where a loss is caused by interruption to the business.

AGGREGATE LIMIT OF INDEMNITY

The maximum amount an insurer will pay under a policy in respect of all accumulated claims arising within a specified period.

ALL-RISKS

Term used to describe insurance against loss of, or damage to, property arising from any cause except those specifically named as being excluded.

ASSURANCE

A term interchangeable with insurance but generally used in connection with life cover as assurance implies the certainty of an event and insurance the possibility of an event happening. For example, death is inevitable, but a fire is not.

AVERAGE

A clause in policies whereby, in the event of under-insurance, the claim paid out by the insurer is restricted to the same proportion of the loss as the sum insured under the policy bears to the total value of the insured item. For example, a building is insured for £100,000 but is worth £200,000. If something destroyed it, insurers would only pay up to 50% of the costs (because they are under-insured), and to a maximum of £100,000.

BUSINESS INTERRUPTION

Loss of profits or revenue, following a material damage loss.

BUSINESS INSURANCE

Cover for business firms, governmental units, or non-profit organisations, to protect against losses through unforeseen circumstances in return for the payment of a premium. See also Travel Insurance for items covered. Employees on a business travel insurance policy may not be individually named, but covered by a blanket policy. May include personal cover for directors.

BUSINESS TRAVEL INSURANCE

Travel insurance which covers business trips, including those where the nature of the personal activity is of a manual nature. Bar work, labouring or simply supervisory or clerical in nature. (See below Travel Insurance)

CANCELLATION

Termination of a policy before it is due to expire. There may be a cancellation clause in a policy setting out the condition under which the policy may be cancelled by notice. The period of notice could be anything from forty-eight hours to three months. In most cases this will cause a refund of premium to be due from the insurer.

CLAIMS

Injury or loss to the insured arising that causes liability to the insurer under a policy it has issued.

CO-INSURANCE PROVISIONS

Where there is a significant and unusual risk (e.g. a warehouse full of butane gas) the insurers might ask the client to pay a percentage of any claim; typically, up to 30%. The insured party might be required to pay a larger than normal excess. For instance, the normal fire excess might be £250, but because a fire alarm is not operative it might be increased to £10,000 until it is working correctly.

COMMERCIAL COMBINED INSURANCE

Several commercial insurances put together as a single package.

COMMERCIAL INSURANCE

Insurance for business firms, governmental units or non-profit organisations to protect against losses through unforeseen circumstances in return for the payment of a premium.

COMMON LAW

Common Law comprises the ancient customs and usages of the land, which have been recognised by the courts and given the force of law. It is a complex system of law, both civil and criminal, although it is greatly modified and extended by statute law and equity. It is unwritten and has come down in the recorded judgements of judges who have interpreted it for hundreds of years.

COMMUNITY COMPANY

An insurance company whose head office is in a member state of the European Economic Community.

CONCEALMENT

Deliberate suppression by a proposer for insurance of a material fact relating to the risk, usually voiding the contract.

CONSEQUENTIAL LOSS

Insurance of loss following direct damage e.g. loss of profits or loss of use insurance.

COVER NOTE

A document issued to the insured confirming details of the insurance cover placed. Some cover notes are a legal requirement, e.g. motor.

DEDUCTIBLE

The specified amount a loss must exceed before a claim is payable. Only the amount in excess of the deductible is recoverable.

DEFERRED PREMIUM

The part of a premium which, following agreement with underwriters, is payable by instalments, usually quarterly or half yearly.

EMPLOYERS' LIABILITY INSURANCE

Insurance by employers regarding their liability to employees for injury or disease arising out of and in the course of their employment. With some exemptions this insurance is compulsory in Great Britain, and can only be provided by an authorised insurer.

ENDORSEMENT

Documentary evidence of a change in the wording of or cover offered by an existing policy or qualification of wording if the policy is written on restricted terms. (See also ADDENDUM).

EXCESS

The first portion of a loss or claim which is borne by the insured. An excess can be either voluntary to obtain premium reduction, or imposed for underwriting reasons.

EXCLUSION

A provision in a policy that excludes the insurer's liability in certain circumstances or for specified types of loss.

EX-GRATIA PAYMENT

A payment made by an insurer to a policyholder where there is no legal liability to pay.

FAMILY FLEET

A motor insurance policy covering all cars in a family and all drivers. Does not necessarily allow all drivers to drive all cars, so a 17-year-old can't drive Dad's Porsche or Mum's Range Rover. Generally there has to be at least one car worth more than £35,000.

FIRST LOSS INSURANCE ARRANGEMENT

Insurance where the sum insured is accepted to be less than the value of the property but the insurer undertakes to pay claims up to the sum insured, without application of a normal average. Any loss above this is borne by the insured. For this reason, the insured will get a reduced premium compared to full cover at full value.

GOODS IN TRANSIT

Loss of goods from stolen vehicles, or goods damaged in transit.

GROSS PREMIUM

A term normally applied to gross written premiums before deduction of brokerage fees and discounts.

HAZARD

A physical or moral feature that introduces or increases the risk.

HIGH NET WORTH

A household policy designed to cover very high values for Buildings normally over £500k, Contents over £75k and extensive valuable items of jewellery, watches, antiques and fine art.

INCEPTION DATE

The date from which the insurer is at risk.

INCREASE IN COST OF WORKING

Under a business interruption policy some cover is provided for additional expenditure incurred by the insured solely for the purpose of reducing the shortage in production following an insured event.

INDEMNITY

A principle whereby the insurer seeks to place the insured in the same position after a loss as they occupied immediately before the loss (as far as possible).

INDEMNITY PERIOD

Under a business interruption insurance the period during which cover is proved for disruption to the business following the occurrence of an insured peril.

INSURABLE INTEREST

For a contract of insurance to be valid the policyholder must have an interest in the insured item that is recognised at law whereby they benefit from its safety, wellbeing or freedom from liability and would be prejudiced by its damage or the existence of liability. This is called the insurable interest and must exist at the time the policy is taken out and at the time of the loss.

INSURABLE VALUE

The value of the insurable interest which the insured has in the insured occurrence or event. It is the amount to be paid out by the insurer (assuming full insurance) in the event of total loss or destruction of the item insured.

INSURANCE BROKER/INTERMEDIARY

An insurance intermediary who advises their clients and arranges their insurances. Although they act as the agent of their client, they are normally remunerated by a commission (brokerage) from the insurer. An insurance broker is a full-time specialist with professional skills in handling insurance business. Since January 2005 intermediaries and brokers must be registered with, and regulated by, the Financial Conduct Authority.

FINANCIAL OMBUDSMAN SERVICE

A bureau established by major insurance companies to oversee the interests of policyholders whose complaints remain unsolved through normal company channels of communication. The service is available to all those holding personal cover with the insurers who have joined the scheme. The decision of the Ombudsman is binding on the insurer, although the insured may appeal to the court if they so wish.

HIGH NET WORTH

A personal insurance covering high buildings and contents values and often incorporating fine art, antiques, and expensive jewellery and other valuable items.

INSURANCE PREMIUM TAX

The Finance Act 1994 introduced this new tax on most general insurance risks located in the UK.

INSURED

The person whose property is insured or in whose favour the policy is issued.

INSURER

An insurance company or Lloyd's underwriter (see Lloyd’s - of London) who, in return for a consideration (a premium) agrees to make good in a manner laid down in the policy any loss or damage suffered by the person paying the premium as a result of some accident or occurrence.

LAPSE

The non-renewal of a policy for any reason.

LATENT DISEASE

An illness which lies dormant for some years before manifesting itself.

LIMIT

The insurer's maximum liability under an insurance, which may be expressed 'per accident', 'per event', 'per occurrence', 'per annum', etc

LLOYD'S (OF LONDON)

A Society, incorporated under Act of Parliament of 1871 and known as the Corporation of Lloyd's, which provides the premises a wide variety of services, administrative staff and other facilities to enable the Lloyds market to carry on insurance business efficiently.

A BROKER OF LLOYD'S

A broker approved by the Council of Lloyd's and thereby entitled to enter the underwriting room at Lloyd's and place business direct with underwriters. Lloyd's brokers must meet the Council of Lloyd's stringent requirements as to integrity and financial stability. They must file annually with the Council of Lloyd's a special accountant's report concerning their financial position.

LOSS

Another term for a claim.

LOSS ADJUSTER

Independent qualified loss adjusters are used by Insurers for their experience and expertise necessary to carry out detailed, and in some instances prolonged, investigations of complex and large losses. Although the adjuster's fees are invariably paid by the insurers, they are an impartial professional person and make their judgement on the amount to be paid in settlement solely on the basis of established market practice. It is their task to negotiate a settlement which is within the terms of the policy and fair to both insured and insurer. Should they not be an expert in a particular discipline that is necessary or desirable to pursue negotiations, they will consult or employ such an expert.

LOSS ASSESSOR

In motor insurance, an engineer. In other classes a person who, in return for a fee (usually a percentage of the amount claimed), acts for the claimant in negotiating the claim.

MATERIAL DAMAGE WARRANTY

A warranty in a business interruption insurance policy stipulating that for the interruption insurance to become effective there must be a policy in force in respect of the material damage and a claim paid or admitted thereunder for such damage caused by an insured peril.

MATERIAL FACT

Any fact which would influence the insurer in accepting or declining a risk or in fixing the premium or terms and conditions of the contract is material and must be disclosed by a proposer, or by the insurer to the insured.

NAME

Another term for an underwriting member of Lloyd's.

NEGLIGENCE

Perhaps the most common form of tort. In Blyth v Birmingham Waterworks Co. (1856) it was defined as 'the omission to do something which a reasonable man guided by those considerations which ordinarily regulate the conduct of human affairs would do, or doing something which a prudent and reasonable man would not do'. Gives rise to civil liability.

NET PREMIUMS

Term variously used to mean gross premiums net of reinsurance premiums payable, or commission, brokerage, taxes, or any combination of these.

NEW FOR OLD

Where insurers agree to pay the cost of property lost or destroyed without deduction for depreciation.

NO CLAIMS BONUS (OR DISCOUNT)

A rebate of premium given to an insured person by an insurer where no claims have been made by that insured. Very common in motor insurance.

NON-DISCLOSURE

The failure by the insured or their broker to disclose a material fact or circumstance to the underwriter before acceptance of the risk.

PASSENGER LIABILITY

The liability of a carrier to passengers.

PERIL

A contingency, of fortuitous happening, which may be covered or excluded by a policy of insurance. For example, fire, theft or flood.

PERIOD OF RISK

The period during which the insurer can incur liability under the terms of the policy.

PERMANENT HEALTH INSURANCE

Term used to describe contracts of insurance providing continuing benefits in the event of prolonged illness or disability.

PERSONAL ACCIDENT & SICKNESS INSURANCE

Insurance for fixed benefits in the event of death or loss of limbs or sight by accident and/or disablement by accident or sickness. Accident and sickness may be insured together or separately.

PERSONAL MONEY

Cover for cash carried on the person, at home, as well as credit cards misused or stolen.

POLICY

A document detailing the terms and conditions applicable to an insurance contract and constituting legal evidence of the agreement to insure. It is issued by an insurer or their representative for the first period of risk. On renewal a new policy may not be issued, although the same conditions would apply and the current wording would be evidence by the renewal receipt.

POLICY HOLDER

The person in whose name the policy is issued. (See also insured and assured).

PREMIUM

The consideration paid for a contract of insurance.

PRE-EXISTING MEDICAL CONDITIONS

You should tell your broker or insurer about any illness you are currently suffering from, or have already had, even in the past. These are known as pre-existing medical conditions. For Private Medical Insurance, you will not normally be covered for these conditions, but for Travel Insurance, the Insurer may be able to offer cover, sometimes for a higher premium.

PRODUCTS LIABILITY INSURANCE

These policies cover the insured's legal liability for bodily injury to persons, or loss of or damage to property caused by defects in goods (including containers) sold, supplied, erected, installed, repaired, treated, manufactured, and/or tested by the insured.

PRODUCT RECALL

Covers the costs of a manufacturer having to recall defective items which could cause injury or damage to customers or may not comply with government regulations. Products are often recalled under statutory legislation or on the direction of a regulatory body.

PROFESSIONAL INDEMNITY INSURANCE

This policy protects a professional man against their legal liability towards third parties for injury, loss, or damage, arising from their own professional negligence or that of their employees.

PROPOSAL FORM

A form sent by an insurer to a person requiring insurance to obtain sufficient information to allow the insurer to decide whether to accept a risk and what conditions to apply if it is accepted.

PUBLIC LIABILITY

Damage or injury caused to members of the public by you or your employees.

QUOTE

A statement by an insurer of the premium they will require for a particular insurance and the terms applying to that quotation.

REINSTATEMENT

Making good after property is damaged. It is usual for settlement to be effected through the payment of a sum of money, but a policy may give either the insured or insurer the option to restore or rebuild instead.

RENEWAL

The process of continuing an insurance from one period of risk to a succeeding one.

RISK

The peril insured against or an individual exposure.

RISK MANAGEMENT

The identification, measurement and economic control of risks that threaten the assets and earnings of a business or other enterprise.

RUN-OFF INSURANCE

Cover that continues after a business has ceased trading, to cover residual liabilities which might still arise from work previously conducted. Normally applies to professional, regulated businesses such as solicitors, accountants, architects, independent financial advisors, insurance brokers, etc. This is most likely in terms of product liability and professional indemnity. It could continue up to the point where claims can no longer legally be made.

SALVAGE

A recovery of all or part of the value of an insured item on which a claim has been paid. The insurer will normally dispose of the item and apply the proceeds to reduce the cost of the claim.

SCHEDULE

The part of a policy containing information peculiar to that particular risk. The greater part of a policy is likely to be identical for all risks within a class of business covered by the same insurer.

STANDARD PERILS

- Fire
- Lightning
- Explosion
- Aircraft
- Riot
- Civil commotion
- Malicious Damage
- Earthquake
- Subterranean Fire

- Storm
- Flood
- Escape of water from tanks or fixed apparatus or pipes
- Escape of oil
- Impact by vehicles or animals
- Sprinkler leakage
- Theft or attempted theft
- Falling trees
- Accidental damage
- Accidental damage to fixed glass
- Subsidence
- Landslip
- Ground heave
- Strikes and labour disturbances
- Collapse of TV aerials
- Sanitary ware (toilets and sinks)
- Underground services

STATEMENT OF FACT

An alternative to a completed proposal form. A statement provided by the insurer clarifying the basis on which insurance is accepted and what conditions apply. Also includes the insurers understanding of the information presented by the insured or their broker when proposing the risk for insurance.

STATUTE LAW

Presently the most important source of law is statute law, otherwise known as Acts of Parliament; which may create entirely new law, over-rule, modify, or extend existing principles of common law and equity, and repeal or modify existing Statute law.

SUBJECT TO SURVEY

Phrase used by an insurer to signify provisional acceptance of an insurance pending inspection by a surveyor whose report is necessary to determine the rate and conditions applicable.

SUM INSURED

The maximum amount payable in the event of a claim under contract of insurance.

THIRD PARTY

A person claiming against an insured. In insurance terminology the first party is the insurer and the second party is the insured.

THIRD PARTY LIABILITY

Liability of the insured to persons who are not parties to the contract of insurance and are not employees of the insured.

TRAVEL INSURANCE

Insurance whilst travelling covering:

- Cancellation
- Medical Expenses
- Personal Accident
- Baggage and valuables
- Personal Money
- Liability for damage or injury to others
- Delayed departure
- Legal expenses
- Ski Trip
- Adventure activities

UNDERLYING INSURANCE

The primary insurance as distinct from excess insurance.

UNDERWRITER

A person who accepts business on behalf of an insurer. (See also Lloyd's underwriter.)

UTMOST GOOD FAITH

Insurance contracts are contracts of utmost good faith (*uberrima fides*), which means both parties to the contract have a duty to disclose clearly and accurately all material facts relating to the proposed insurance. Any breach of this duty by the proposer may entitle the insurer to repudiate liability.

WARRANTY

A very strict condition in a policy imposed by an insurer. A breach entitles the insurer to deny liability. Since the 2015 Fair Presentation Regulations insurers can only deny a claim where the warranty is *specific* to a claim. For instance, the lack of an approved alarm in a theft claim, whereas previously they could deny any claim, where *any* warranty was violated.

WEAR AND TEAR

This is the amount deducted from claims payments to allow for any depreciation in the property insured which is caused by its normal usage. Unless the provision of new for old applies.

WITHOUT PREJUDICE

Term used in discussion and correspondence. Where there is a dispute or negotiations for a settlement and terms are offered 'without prejudice', an offer so made or a letter so marked and subsequent correspondence cannot be admitted in evidence without the consent of both parties concerned.

Term also used by an underwriter when paying a claim which they feel may not attach to the policy. This payment must not be treated as a precedent for future similar claims.

1

THE REGULATORY ENVIRONMENT

The regulation of general insurance is dealt with by several organisations in the United Kingdom. It is essential that any person buying insurance cover has a rudimentary understanding of how the industry is regulated. Only in this way will they recognise the markers that set the professional and compliant organisations aside from those who act illegally or fraudulently.

There are 'ghost' insurers and brokers (online mainly), who appear credible (and cheap) but are fronts for criminal organisations who will steal your money. The documents provided will look real, but are fake. If the police stop you, in the case of motor insurance, you may still be prosecuted for having no insurance. This knowledge will also allow you to ask prudent questions about an organisation's status and it will allow you to search various registers to establish if the companies you are talking to are real and properly regulated and compliant in the United Kingdom.

Regulatory organisations start at the highest level; dealing with large-scale issues of the economy, such as banks and international trading. Then, moving down through the tiers of the industry and, finally, dealing with the products and purchases of individual businesses and private consumers

> ***Quick Tip***
>
> If you are ever unsure about the status of an insurer or broker, or if the price quoted appears ridiculously cheap compared to others, then look for another way to contact them. Find another website for the company and call a different number to check them out. See PRA and FCA, below.

THE BANK OF ENGLAND (BOE)

Founded in 1694, the Bank of England is the central bank of the United Kingdom. The Bank's mission is to promote the good of the people of the United Kingdom by maintaining monetary and financial stability. They are politically independent of the Government.

www.bankofengland.co.uk/Pages/home.aspx

PRUDENTIAL REGULATORY AUTHORITY (PRA)

The Prudential Regulation Authority (PRA) was created as a part of the Bank of England by the Financial Services Act (2012) and is responsible for the prudential regulation and supervision of around 1,700 banks, building societies, credit unions, insurers, and major investment firms. The PRA's objectives are set out in the Financial Services and Markets Act 2000 (FSMA).

www.bankofengland.co.uk/pra/Pages/default.aspx

FINANCIAL CONDUCT AUTHORITY (FCA)

The FCA aims to ensure financial markets work and consumers get a fair deal. This means ensuring the financial industry is run with integrity, firms provide consumers with appropriate products and services, and consumers can trust that firms have their best interests at heart.

It regulates over 70,000 businesses. The FCA is accountable to the Treasury (responsible for the UK's financial system) and Parliament.

www.fca.org.uk

INSURANCE OMBUDSMAN'S SERVICE (IOS)

The IOS was set up by Parliament to sort out individual complaints consumers and financial businesses aren't able to resolve themselves. This service is free to consumers.

Nine out of ten people say they have no complaints with their bank, insurer or finance firm, and most financial transactions take place with no problems. Sometimes things go wrong and when they do, and a customer isn't happy, it's up to the business to resolve it. The business must be given the chance to investigate a problem – and they have eight weeks to do so.

If the customer is still dissatisfied, they can go to the IOS who will listen to both sides of the story and be honest. The ombudsman will give advice or decide based on the facts presented. The ombudsman won't take sides and will look at every problem with an open mind.

www.financial-ombudsman.org.uk

THE FINANCIAL SERVICES COMPENSATION SCHEME

The FSCS is the UK's statutory fund of last resort for customers of financial services firms. This means that FSCS can pay compensation to consumers if a financial services firm is unable, or likely to be unable, to pay claims against it. The FSCS is an independent body, set up under the Financial Services and Markets Act 2000 (FSMA). They do not charge consumers for using the service.

The FSCS covers business conducted by UK authorised firms, the FCA and PRA. European firms (authorised by their home state regulator) that operate in the UK may also be covered.

The FSCS was established to assist private individuals, although small businesses are also covered. Large businesses are generally excluded although there are some exceptions to this for deposit and insurance claims.

www.fscs.org.uk

> ***Quick Tip***
>
> By checking the websites of the various organisations above, you should at first sight be able to check whether the organisation you are dealing with is real and credible. Beware, cloning can happen, and it is wise to cross-check with other registers, such as Companies House, and ensure the registered addresses and websites are real and in the UK. If you are unsure, ring the customer helpline of either the ABI or BIBA (see next chapter).

2

PROFESSIONAL BODIES & ASSOCIATIONS

There are several professional bodies in the United Kingdom that strive to uphold the highest standards within their membership. That a company is a member of one of these organisations, whilst not a guarantee of perfection, is a reasonable pointer you are dealing with a real company properly regulated and authorised in the UK.

ASSOCIATION OF BRITISH INSURERS (ABI)

The ABI is the voice of the UK's insurance and long-term savings industry. A productive, inclusive and thriving sector, it provides peace of mind to households and businesses across the UK, and powers the growth of local and regional economies by enabling trade, risk taking, investment, and innovation.

www.abi.org.uk

BRITISH INSURANCE BROKERS ASSOCIATION (BIBA)

The British Insurance Brokers' Association is the UK's leading general insurance intermediary organisation representing the interests of insurance brokers, intermediaries, and their customers.

BIBA membership includes nearly 2,000 regulated firms employing more than 100,000 staff between them. General insurance brokers contribute 1% of GDP to the UK economy, and they arrange 52% of all general insurance and 78% of all commercial business.

Insurance brokers put a client's interests first, providing advice, access to suitable cover, and risk management.

www.biba.org.uk

CHARTERED INSURANCE INSTITUTE (CII)

The Chartered Insurance Institute is the world's largest professional body for people working in insurance and financial services.

Based in the UK for over 100 years, they are a uniquely global institute, known and respected worldwide. They have over 120,000 members in over 150 countries, and are widely regarded as the standard bearer for ethical business in all areas of the insurance profession, for those working in the life and pensions sector, or for mortgage or financial advisers.

www.cii.co.uk

OTHER ORGANISATIONS

There are many other professional bodies in the UK that relate to specific industry sectors, regional or local associations, and groups of insurance professionals. In most cases the members will also belong to one or more of the bodies above.

Other professional organisations such as The Law Society, The Association of Chartered Certified Accountants, and the Royal Institute of Chartered Surveyors, arrange certain insurance permissions for their members. Membership confers authorisation with the relevant regulatory authority, normally the FCA.

3

INSURANCE REQUIRED BY LAW

It is worth understanding what insurance cover is legally required in the UK and without which you may break the law. In the United Kingdom there are only two compulsory insurances.

MOTOR VEHICLE INSURANCE

Cover for injury or damage to other people or property whilst driving a motor vehicle. This is often referred to as Road Traffic Act cover. In practice, few insurers will offer this basic cover, other than for some forms of road-going plant and equipment. Most vehicle cover is Third Party, Fire and Theft (for older, less valuable vehicles) or Comprehensive cover (including accidental damage to your own vehicle).

EMPLOYERS' LIABILITY INSURANCE

Required under the terms of the Employers' Liability (Compulsory Insurance) Act 1969. Cover is required to protect employees who may be injured or get ill whilst working.

The minimum cover under the act is £5,000,000, but in practice most insurers give cover up to £10,000,000.

They restrict it to the lower level for acts of terrorism.

This requirement applies to all businesses who have employees, including voluntary or unpaid workers, labour-only sub-contractors and directors in limited companies. This requirement applies regardless of how frequently the employees work for the company.

The only businesses that do not require this cover are unincorporated companies, where there are principals only and no one else employed. A principal can't sue themselves, so cover isn't required.

PENALTIES

If you do not have Road Traffic Act cover for a vehicle, you are likely to get a hefty fine and at least six points on your licence. Subsequent or more serious offences will cause the award of more points, larger fines, and lengthier bans. Sometimes you may they may require you to re-take your driving test before they restore your licence.

With Employers' Liability Insurance, because an employee could be injured and disabled for life, or worse die and leave a family to fend for itself, the penalties can be high. Fines can be up to £2,500 per day and prison sentences of up to six months. If they bring more serious charges, directors guilty of presiding over corporate manslaughter could find themselves in jail for years.

INSPECTIONS

Whilst not an insurance, statutory inspection of certain plant and machinery is required by law under:

- PUWER - Provision of Use of Work regulations 1998
- LOLER – Lift Operations & Lifting & Handling Regulations 1998
- PSSR – Pressure Systems Safety Regulations 2000
- COSHH – Care of Substances Hazardous to Health
- HACCP – Hazard Analysis & Critical Control Point

This is to ensure the equipment is safe and will not injure employees or the public. Inspections can be provided by the engineering departments of insurance companies, or specialist engineering service providers.

RECOMMENDED BUT NOT MANDATORY

No other insurances are required by law but many are advisable for the protection of the business. One of the main reasons for using a broker is to obtain professional advice about the risks to obtain cover. It was my aim when writing this book to give guidance in that direction, but this does not replace a serious discussion with a professional about your specific situation, needs and requirements. Every business is different and requires a bespoke solution.

4

TAX ON GENERAL INSURANCES

There are two Taxes routinely applied in the insurance industry in the United Kingdom.

- Insurance Premium Tax (IPT)
- Value Added Tax (VAT)

These taxes are added to the relevant contracts, after the premium has been calculated by the insurance company. Where a commission is paid to the broker, tax is liable on that element as well. They are then levied on the brokers account (if there is one) and then to the insured as a total premium.

The insurance premium, minus any commission, is paid to the insurer, who remits the tax to the UK government and treasury. Note: these rates are correct at time of publication and subject to variation.

- IPT on all general insurances is 12%
- IPT on travel insurance is 20%
- VAT on all inspection contracts of service is 20%
- Some elements of Marine Cargo Insurance are exempt from UK tax.

Quick Tip

When you pay your premium to a broker you are paying Insurance Premium Tax (IPT) at 12% *including* his commission.

If your broker takes 0% commission and charges a fee instead, you see if their earnings are reasonable.

You also don't pay tax on their fee as IPT doesn't apply to professional fees.

5

THE UK MARKETPLACE

If you are to make an intelligent decision about the purchase of insurance, you need to understand something of the marketplace in which you make that purchase. In the UK you have three choices. You can buy direct from an insurer, direct from the scheme provider of a single product, or you can approach a broker who will compare various products.

> ***Quick Tip***
>
> When you buy direct (often online) you won't receive advice about the suitability of the product for your needs, just an explanation of the product.

When you deal with a broker, they should complete a detailed fact find so they can understand your situation. Thereafter they should approach several insurers on your behalf to match your needs to a suitable product at the best price they can achieve. Once they have sourced the correct solution, they will present their recommendation to you in a formal written document, along with full terms and conditions. They should take time to explain this to you in simple terms – the clauses, conditions, warranties, endorsements, and exclusions that apply to the recommended policies.

The marketplace in which you will make your purchase is split as follows:

- London Market
- Lloyd's of London
- Insurance Companies
- Insurance Aggregators
- Insurance Intermediaries (Brokers)

LONDON MARKET

Within a square mile, there is a concentration of the major global insurers such as; Allianz, AXA, Aviva, RSA and Zurich, and many niche specialists and leading international re-insurers from across the globe. Many global broking businesses such as Marsh, AON, Lockton, and Willis also have presences in London. To be in one place allows them all an unprecedented ability to talk to one another, co-ordinate work and projects, and meet face to face. Therefore, London continues to be the single most important city in the world for the provision of insurance.

LLOYD'S OF LONDON

As an individual you will never deal directly with Lloyd's of London, they do not permit it. You may have insurance arranged by a broker or scheme provider that is backed by syndicates at Lloyd's. If you look in your policy wording for the identity of insurers you may see something like ‘Certain Underwriters at Lloyd’s’ or the actual name and number of a syndicate there.

Lloyd’s of London is a marketplace that works in tandem with a corporation. The corporation provides governance, rules and guidelines about how the market should operate. It also provides analysis, information, reports, and supports the members of the market and seeks to maintain the reputation of the market.

Specialist underwriters, normally organised as syndicates, put a price on the risks presented to them. They feed lots of this business into the market by brokers of Lloyd’s, cover holders, and other independent broking businesses. The concentration of expertise in the market ensures the pricing and strategy is professional, sustainable, and competitive.

The capital that backs the market is subscribed to by individuals and organisations. Famously, Lloyd’s Names (individual investors who are looking to get a return on the investment they make from underwriting profits) also risk losing their entire personal fortune without limit.

Modernisation is taking place to the practices and procedures of the market and in its ability to deliver documentation quickly under current regulations. Work is constantly undertaken to ensure the financial viability of the syndicates and insurers that operate there, for the benefit of the market and the policyholders. The Bank of England and the Prudential Regulation Authority have oversight here.

Working under the Lloyd’s banner, the market and the corporation continue to provide a global brand trusted worldwide. They write many of the most complicated and valuable risks. These include the global oil and petroleum industry, worldwide marine cargo, bulk cargo vessels, mining, precious metals and gems, celebrity insurances, massive commercial property development, global corporate businesses and the space industry.

www.lloyds.com

INSURANCE COMPANIES

These come in all shapes and sizes. What they do depends on their target market and the classes of business they are authorised in. Some transact primarily personal insurances such as car, home, and travel, whilst others transact commercial insurances as well. A further group operate limited classes of business and are classed as niche insurers. Good examples are insurers providing credit guarantee, contingency bonds, professional indemnity, marine cargo and engineering damage covers.

Some deal directly with the public and do not deal with brokers, such as Direct Line and Admiral, whilst others deal with brokers, but also have direct arms operating under different brands. A good example is RSA, whose direct arm is More Than. AVIVA operates under their name to brokers and direct customers alike.

Where insurers deal with brokers they do this at different levels and across all geographic areas. They may give brokers access to a standard product range but they have better deals and products for large brokers and broker networks. These schemes have dedicated underwriting teams and are at preferential rates.

Where insurers deal directly with the public, the

types of insurance they transact are for simple policies for cars, homes, travel, shops, offices, or for property owners. These are package policies where a uniform market need is served.

If your business is large enough, and I mean very large, you might access insurers direct in the London market. You need sufficient in-house management with the right experience to interact with insurers at this level. Organisations like British Petroleum (BP), British Telecom (BT), Shell (UK) and Sky Broadcasting would be big enough.

There are also international reinsurers like Swiss-Re, who provide reinsurance to insurance companies. Reinsurance spreads risk across the globe, so the total cost of a claim never falls on any one insurer in isolation. This is important when significant global events occur. In all cases the costs of such events are too massive to be handled by one insurer, or even a number in one country. International re-insurers bear the cost across the globe. Insurance allows international trade to prosper and ride through difficult and challenging events and times. As a customer you will never deal with re-insurers.

INSURANCE AGGREGATORS

Insurance aggregators enter into agreements with several insurers, direct or otherwise, to pass them business through a price comparison website. The client enters their information into an online quote system which is transmitted to the insurers. Insurers then return quotes via the aggregator's site. comparethemarket.com is typical of an aggregator in action. They present customers with several quotes, ranked in price order.

If you go behind the individual quotes, you will often find there are significant differences between terms of cover and what you asked for. Excesses differ markedly, regardless of what you request as do the provision of things like courtesy cars, legal expenses, money cover, goods in transit, and business interruption. On a property owner's policy, it might be the provision of emergency response callout or the level of public liability.

Where there are several products from the same brand, the cheapest might be a stripped-down version with low limits of cover.

What they return to you is the nearest equivalent policy each insurer has available to your original request or the only solution they have. They give the illusion of choice but in reality you are buying what is on the shelf whether or not it's right for you. The shelf does not contain all the products available in the marketplace. Direct Line and Admiral, for instance, make great play on the fact they are not on aggregator's sites. But you will find that these aren't necessarily the cheapest prices available in the market. Other routes may provide better value for money. Affinity sites for organisations with similar interest often have better deals; for example, MG Owners Club, Caravan Club, alarm installers, and charities, to name but a few.

> ***Quick Tip***
>
> If you do business direct with an insurer or single product provider, you are not receiving independent advice about suitability or the adequacy of the cover provided. Should a claim fail, you are likely to be dealing with that situation on your own, without independent support.

INSURANCE BROKERS

The UK insurance market is diverse. Virtually nowhere else in the world is there the sheer number of brokers we have in the UK, servicing all kinds of needs and markets. The UK also has a law of agency, which again has few parallels anywhere else in the rest of the world, and has fostered a unique relationship to develop between brokers, insurers and customers. This has allowed a vibrant marketplace to emerge right across the UK. In most other countries agents act for one insurer only, in a particular city or town. In the UK we have five classes of insurance brokers, they are:

- Local
- Regional
- National
- Lloyd's
- International

LOCAL BROKERS

Local brokers are normally found in one town. They often have only one office and their activities are often confined to a small area surrounding that town. If they are on the high street in a small town, they are most likely dealing with the personal needs and the small commercial enterprises within that area. If they rely largely on walk-in traffic for their business, they will most likely have a high proportion of personal insurances such as car, household, travel and pet insurance, and small package business covers such as property owners, shops and offices. This reflects the needs of customers in their location. They are unlikely to have developed a response for or skills in complex commercial business, unless they have acquired a member of staff with those skills living in the area.

REGIONAL BROKERS

Regional brokers come in two distinct versions. They are those with several offices dotted over a particular region. Higos Insurance Services (now owned by GRP) was and is a perfect example of a broker with over twenty offices spread across the South West of England, as is Thomas Carrols in South Wales. The offices will deal with personal insurances and package business in each branch, but call upon specialist staff to deal with more complex business. Personnel will operate across the region for their business.

The second model is of a specialist broker, normally in more complex commercial markets, who may only have one or two offices, but may have customers across a region or across the whole of the UK. My business Severn Bay Corporate Solutions is a perfect example of this. Our head office is in Cardiff, South Wales, but we have a presence in the London market at least two days a week and clients all over the UK. We have clients in Wales naturally, because they find us by reputation and we market locally, but also in the North West, North East, Midlands, Suffolk, London and the Home Counties. We also have some very large clients, with complex commercial businesses turning over £100m+ per annum.

Brokers in this second category might transact a wide range of commercial business types or may operate a scheme business for a specific industry and have negotiated covers for that sector. Because of this and their reputations, they may attract business direct from customers in that industry, from right across the UK, but they may provide their services to other brokers in local brokerages (see above), who wish to place business on the scheme for their customers. This is called sub-broking and is a routine feature of the insurance market in the UK. A good example of this is Sutton Specialist Risks, who place business for alarm and security companies, the commercial cleaning sector, pest controllers, renewable energy, and the aviation industry.

BROKER NETWORKS

These exist to give smaller brokers the buying power of larger ones. They are formed to bring a large book of business to the market, attractive to insurers. On the back of the total book of business, higher levels of commission are available, which would not have been available to the individual broker. It is however not all about increased income. The networks charge their members for a range of services such as, managing client premium trust accounts, insurer account reconciliation, compliance, training, but most of all, access to markets, schemes and products.

The offerings are usually distinct and fit what the individual broker wants. Some have large personal lines solutions, whilst others are predominantly for commercial brokers. Good examples here are Compass, Momentum, Broker Network, Bluefin Partnership, Marsh Pro-Broker, Willis Networks and the Purple Partnership. Some of these names are large brokers in their own right and can therefore leverage a high level of service for their members, including dedicated underwriting teams and facilities.

Generally, the member remains completely independent and able to place business where they please. In some networks however, the placing strategy is more proscriptive and certain classes of business must be placed in network facilities with very little room for manoeuvre. It is therefore essential to ask your broker in all circumstances who they intend to approach, so you can understand who has considered your business.

NATIONAL BROKERS

These brokers have offices in all major towns and cities across the UK. They will transact personal and commercial insurances and will often have London-based broking teams. They may have niche teams dedicated to certain types of insurance. They look to place any kind of business to grow and expand their business. Good examples are; Arthur J Gallagher's, Jelf, Swinton, Bluefin and CCV. All have high street offices across the UK and all can be approached directly by members of the public. Sometimes they sub-broker products to other brokers.

BROKERS FOR LLOYD'S

These brokers are a special category all to themselves. They are authorised to enter the Lloyd's building and approach syndicates to arrange insurances for their customers or for other non-Lloyd's brokers who have approached them.

They may enter the market to place individual risks, fill up scheduled slips where a lead syndicate takes the first and normally most substantial stake in a risk, to be followed by other syndicates taking small portions of the risk until the slip is 100% underwritten. Lloyd's placing brokers have extensive knowledge of which syndicates are writing what types of business and know who will lead and who will follow on any class of business. This is vital when placing business at Lloyd's as capacity to transact business in the market can change almost daily. This is often driven by financial markets and access to capital.

Lloyd's brokers also go into the market to secure capacity for schemes they manage, and whilst they are always looking for long-term support for their schemes, capacity can change dependent of the syndicate's risk profile and profitability. It is not unusual for a syndicate to withdraw and be replaced by another from time to time.

Lloyd's brokers are not open to the public and most their business is passed to them by other brokers. In this way the Lloyd's broker is taking a professional presentation to market and they build a relationship with that broker as they have to trust that the information presented is full and accurate. They may ask for additional information to satisfy the needs of the syndicates they approach.

Good examples are Miles Smith, Carrol Holman's, Jardine Lloyd Thompson, Anglo Pacific, Bennet Gould and RJ Langman. They may be securing capacity for their own schemes or looking to place individual risks for other brokers.

INTERNATIONAL BROKERS

Within the London market, nationally and regionally, a variety of global brokers have a presence such as Marsh, AON, Willis, Lockton's and Arthur J. Gallagher. As global brokers they take advantage of business they can write within the UK and maintain a presence in London for global risks. They often maintain a Lloyd's broking arm to allow them to negotiate very large risks on their own behalf, or on the behalf of brokers who bring business to them.

> ***Quick Tip***
>
> Ask your broker whether they place risks in the London market and what relationships they have. If they have direct relationships with Lloyd's brokers, then you can reasonably expect they have sufficient experience in more complex risks. If they place cover via another broker, then that may be the broker you need to speak to.

6

DIFFERENT BUSINESSES' NEEDS

Businesses can be divided into four main types, defined by their main priority. If you look at your own business, you'll see it fits, in broad terms, within one of these:

- Businesses based in commercial premises
- Contractors working away from their premises
- Professional Advisors and Service Providers
- Charities, Social Service and Community Interest Companies.

BUSINESS BASED IN COMMERCIAL PREMISES: 'STUFF AND TRUCKS'

These businesses are primarily concerned with the protection of physical assets such as buildings, equipment, machinery, and stock. It is these assets that create revenue. They are things you can count, see, and touch, and have value.

Lots of these businesses will be found on industrial estates and include manufacturing, engineering, warehousing, distribution, and wholesalers. It also includes lots of retail businesses on the high street, whose stock is valuable, such as jewellers, clothiers, and electronics.

They may have fleets of vehicles including cars, vans and heavy goods vehicles to deliver their own goods or the goods of others.

They will need liability cover, but their primary concern is the physical assets they need to protect.

CONTRACTORS WORKING AWAY FROM THEIR PREMISES: 'HARD HATS AND HIGH-VIZ'

These businesses are primarily concerned with their liabilities and the claims that might be made against them by the people they work for, in case they do damage or cause injury on their premises. They may not even be allowed to work on a customer's site without liability cover.

This is probably the most diverse business sector including all those men and women you find on building sites. It includes; ground workers, steel erectors, crane operators, ventilation, air conditioning, concrete layers, plumbers, electricians, lighting contractors, and many, many more. This is only a small list of the trades that might work away from their own premises.

These businesses might have their own premises and vehicles, and they may do some work there, but their focus is doing work for other people at their locations. As the self-employed sector grows, contractors can now include IT professionals, marketing consultants and other service-orientated professionals.

PROFESSIONAL ADVISORS AND SERVICE PROVIDERS: 'THE SUITS'

These people mainly work in offices and visit their customers at their premises. Their main concern, in insurance terms, is the claims they might face for failing to do what they were paid to do; professional negligence.

If a client suffers a financial loss then alleges that it resulted from negligence, errors, or omissions of the advisor, they will make a claim to recover those losses. It is in this area that professional indemnity cover is required. It can extend to anyone providing a service on which others rely. For instance, electricians carrying out inspections and testing.

This business category is also diverse. It includes traditional professional classes like architects, solicitors, surveyors, accountants, independent financial advisers (IFAs), insurance brokers, public relations consultants, marketing companies, HR consultants, web developers, and social media gurus. Once again, this is far from an exhaustive list.

CHARITIES AND SOCIAL SERVICE PROVIDERS: 'CARERS'

These organisations are out there doing tireless work for no profit, funded either by government grants, private donations, or a mixture of both.

They provide essential services and fulfil contracts awarded by local authorities, such as domiciliary care, drug abuse, homelessness and mental care.

Charities and social care providers may also fall into the three categories above if they operate facilities or shops, providing services in the community, working on other people's premises, or providing advice and guidance to individuals or other organisations. It also includes many associated training bodies working alongside local government and charities.

RICH VARIETY

These are broad generalisations and there is a great deal of overlap. Manufacturers may have teams that work away on installations, providing maintenance and repairs. Businesses that work away may have yards to store equipment, plant and machinery, and office-based advisory services may send consultants out to work on the premises of their clients.

The four broad classes of business give you a starting point to determine the main priorities for cover, but complexity is never far away and a detailed analysis of the activities of a business is essential to determine the range of cover that will be required.

Attention to detail is everything at this stage, so use "What if?" questions to take you beyond what is obvious, to keep asking questions, until they run out. A simple set are:

- Who?
- When?
- Where?
- What is it?
- What is it doing?
- What are you doing about it?

And at each stage ask: What If? What If? What if? So What? So What? So What?... until you run out of things to ask.

You need to discover the subtle nuances in your

business and the best way to do this is open the mind of the person who set it up, and whose passion and vision carry it forward. If that's you, then it should be relatively easy, otherwise talk to the boss or a senior director. That's where you will find the information required to understand what you need to protect.

It is often said turnover is vanity, profit is sanity, and cashflow is king. Protecting things you can see is simple, but business interruption and loss of revenue are the first complex factors that must be understood. Without an income flow the business can't pay the running costs and wages. Staff will leave, and after that a business will quickly cease to trade.

> ***Quick Tip***
>
> Buying the services of a claims adjustor to help settle your claim after serious damage can be expensive. It could cost 10-20% of the final settlement, and that could be thousands. Bought in advance as an insurance it can cost as little as £35 a year. This is one of the best insurance add-ons you can buy if you own property or have valuable equipment. It is a simple way to get your claim settled quickly and your business up and running with minimum disruption.

UNINCORPORATED BUSINESSES

When you start your business, you may set up as a sole trader, which is an individual person, using a trading name as the face of their business. For example, Fred Jones t/a Fred Jones Builders. (t/a means trading as)

This is an unincorporated business. In law, the business and the person are inseparable. They are the same for all purposes, including tax and VAT. The business is treated as the individual and income is personal income of the individual, so tax is paid personally on all the income of the business. Eligible costs can be set against the income.

The owner(s) are called Principals and there are no shares. By agreement they may set out an agreement that states who owns what percentage of the business, its assets, liabilities, and profits. Because there is no difference legally between the principals and the business, they are not employees of the business.

INCORPORATED BUSINESSES

As a business grows and the assets and liabilities become greater, the business might become incorporated, or put into a form where the business is legally separate from the individual(s) running it. They now become directors or partners. One director, or another person, is normally given the title of Company Secretary and has the responsibility for filing accounts and other returns with Companies House. A company such as this might be called something like Fred Jones Builders Limited.

The most important thing to note here is that an incorporated business becomes a legal entity in its own right, separate from the individuals who set it up, own it, and run it. This is done to protect the owners from the worst consequences of failure. Should the business fail they can, under certain circumstances, walk away from the losses and debts.

There are now shareholders and the percentage of

their shares denote the limit of their liabilities. Most companies have a paid up share capital; the amount of money used to start the business when it was registered (incorporated). It represents what each person put in on day one and it is nominally the limit of their liability. It can be as low as £100.

> ***Quick Tip***
>
> If the directors or partners call an end to trading activity, cease trading, and incur no additional costs, when they are aware of circumstances that mean the business can't continue, then they are probably safe from the liabilities and debts of the business. However, if they continue to trade past the point it is reasonable to do so, they may be liable.

PARTNERSHIPS

General partnerships are governed by the Partnership Act of 1890. A partnership does not constitute a separate legal entity from the individual partners. Partnerships are not required to pay income tax; each partner files the profits or losses of the business on their personal income tax return.

General partners have unlimited liability for the debts of the partnership, while limited partners do not. Limited partners (much like shareholders of a corporation) cannot lose an amount greater than their investment in the partnership.

A mixed partnership or Limited Liability Partnership (LLP) includes both individuals and limited companies as partners. However, individual partners who are not directors or shareholders in the limited company partnership will not be affected.

A disadvantage of such a structure is that liability for the debts of the business is unlimited. Each partner is jointly and severally liable, so each partner could find themselves liable for all of the debts if another absconds, not just their share.

PUBLIC COMPANIES

You may wish to convert to a PLC, a Public Limited Company. The main reason for this is to gain a listing on a stock exchange so investment can be sought in the form of shares.

At this point the directors have a higher degree of personal responsibility, because they now have shareholders to whom they owe a duty of care. Their primary concern is to create profits that can be distributed to those shareholders.

CONSEQUENCES OF ARRANGING INSURANCE

The main concern is always the requirement for Employers' Liability insurance before anything else as this is mandatory. In this respect you need to understand who is and who is not legally considered an employee.

TYPES OF CONTRACTORS AND EMPLOYEES

This is probably the most frequent conversation I have with clients. It revolves around the people they bring into their business to do work and whether they should be considered employees, and whether Employers' Liability cover is required.

In an unincorporated company the principal or principals are not employees. If there are no other employees, Employers' Liability cover is not required.

> ***Quick Tip***
>
> If you own several limited companies, as separate legal entities they must be insured separately. They cannot share the same liability cover, as one company cannot be responsible for the liabilities of another. Having them on one policy would make it impossible to separate individual liabilities. The only way to have them on one policy is to have a Holding Company, where subsidiaries are wholly-owned by it. The holding company becomes the named insured and subsidiaries are listed on the policy.

In an incorporated business directors are definitely employees of the business and Employers' Liability cover is required, even if there are no other employees. A Company Secretary is an employee whether or not they are paid.

The only exception is where the company only has one director and no other employees. In these circumstances Employers' Liability cover is not required. It would be difficult to prove that the company was liable for putting that person in a situation where they were injured, if no other person instructed their actions. It the company employs just one other person, Employers'

Liability cover is required. We will cover what 'employment' means shortly.

General partnerships follow the rules for unincorporated businesses, whilst Limited Liability Partnerships follow the rules for incorporated companies.

By the very nature of their size, PLCs always have employees, in fact they are likely to have thousands, therefore Employers' Liability cover is required.

DIRECT EMPLOYEES

These are the ones who are 'on the books'. You calculate their wages, deduct tax, national insurance and auto enrolment payments and remit them directly to the tax authorities and the pension companies, before paying them their net wages. These people are definitely employees, and Employers' Liability cover is required.

BONA FIDE SUB-CONTRACTORS (BFSC)

These are often limited companies that tender for work. They may perform functions with qualifications and accreditations for specific work. Examples include electrical contractors, Gas Safe engineers, crane operators, scaffolders, etc.

They bring their own employees to the job, their own tools and equipment and almost always supply the materials to complete the job. Most importantly they will have their own employers', public, and products liability cover. Finally, they will invoice you for the work that they do. They are not your employees.

VOLUNTEERS AND UNPAID INTERNS

You might rightly think that there is no way these people are your employees and in strict terms, you are correct.

You are not paying them; they may have turned up just this once or may only be working for you for a short period of time to gain work experience and may have been introduced by an academic institution that has a closer relationship with them.

They must, however, be considered as your employee for insurance purposes. If they are working for you, you are responsible for their health and safety. If they are minors (14-17 years) it is even more important you let your insurers know of their presence.

LABOUR-ONLY SUB-CONTRACTORS (LOSC)

The law is clear, if all someone brings to the job is themselves and a bag of tools, then they are considered to be your employee whilst they work for you. They are still to be considered as your employee for insurance purposes, whether self-employed and paying their own tax and National Insurance or not. Even if they have their own insurance it is likely to be public liability only and will not cover them as an employee. If they work on your site, you are responsible for their health and safety and you will require Employers' Liability cover.

SELF-EMPLOYED SUB-CONTRACTORS

These people generally come in to your business to carry out a project or a specific piece of work. It they are not set up as limited companies, then you need to consider if they are your responsibility for Employers' Liability purposes.

In these circumstances, if they are doing manual labour on a site you control, then you should always consider them as a LOSC as above. If they are supervisors, managers, or office-based professionals then it's more complicated. They may have public liability cover, they may even have professional indemnity cover, but they are unlikely to have Employers' Liability cover, but does that mean they are your employees? In these circumstances there are other tests.

Are you the only person they work for? If the answer is yes, consider them your employee but if they work for other people this is a fair sign they do not consider themselves anyone's employee.

Do they produce an invoice for the work done? If they do, this is again a sign they do not consider themselves your employee and may carry out work for other people.

Do they have their own insurance? If they have Public Liability and Employers' Liability cover then they obviously do not consider themselves your employee. If they have professional indemnity cover, the same probably applies.

> ***Quick Tip***
>
> It is essential that you get this right. Failure to arrange Employers' Liability cover where required can lead to fines of up to £2,500 per day. In extreme circumstances (if someone is injured or killed) six months in jail could be imposed upon principals or directors.

7

CLASSES OF INSURANCE

When purchasing insurance for your business there are things you must have, things that are required for specific circumstances, and things which are nice to have as additional protection if they are affordable.

ESSENTIALS

PROPERTY DAMAGE

Damage to buildings, contents, stock, machinery, etc, whilst at a defined premises or away from that premises anywhere in the world.

BUSINESS INTERRUPTION

Loss of profits or revenue, following a property damage loss.

PUBLIC LIABILITY

Damage or injury caused to members of the public by you or your employees.

PRODUCTS LIABILITY

Damage or injury caused to users by the product that you sell, supply or manufacture.

EMPLOYERS' LIABILITY

Damage or injury suffered by your employees, during their employment. Required by law.

COMMERCIAL MOTOR

Can be arranged for individual business use cars and commercial vehicles, or where there are in excess of five vehicles as a fleet insurance. Fleets can contain a mixture of cars, vans, HGVs and special type motorised vehicles. Required by law.

SPECIFIC SITUATIONS

CONTINGENCY BONDS

These can be arranged for a one-off or annual payment depending on the situation and can be arranged for almost any scenario where a financial loss may occur. Examples are for restrictive covenants, lost deeds, HMRC VAT deferments, or contract performance situations. These are sometimes known as financial guarantees.

CONTRACT WORKS

Covers the subject matter of a contract until completion. For example, a house being built, in case it is damaged before it is handed over. It would also cover materials on site, contractor's plant, equipment, and tools, as well as hired plant and equipment. Site huts, portable toilets would also be covered in this example.

CREDIT GUARANTEE

This cover is arranged to pay the bad debts of a policy holder's customers whose businesses fail. This is a financial backstop to an alert service aimed at getting policy holders to reduce their exposure to customers in financial difficulty. Often used in the construction industry where large sums of money can be spent before payment is forthcoming from the end client.

DIRECTORS' AND OFFICERS' LIABILITY

This covers the individual employees who act as a director or other officer within an incorporated business for wrongful acts carried out during their employment, where the incident was unintentional.

EMPLOYEE BENEFITS

This groups several covers together that are usually arranged separately, but can also be arranged by individual:

- Private medical benefits
- Personal accident insurance
- Travel cover
- Death in service life assurance
- Permanent health insurance
- Income protection

ENGINEERING COVER

This can include statutory inspections of equipment, damage to equipment, breakdown of equipment and computers, deterioration of frozen food, cover whilst the equipment is being moved and commissioned, amongst others. There are other covers, but all rely on there being a piece of equipment that is either damaged, breaks down or requires inspection and testing by law. As some of these covers are services rather than insurances, they are subject to 20% VAT not 12% IPT.

GOODS IN TRANSIT

Loss of goods from stolen vehicles or goods damaged in vehicles that are involved in accidents whilst carrying goods. This can cover your own goods in your own vehicles, your goods in a haulier's vehicle or a customer's goods in your vehicles.

LEGAL EXPENSES

Provides legal helplines, legal expenses, and defends you from a range of legal suits which might be brought against you and are not covered above. These can include HR disputes, tax investigations, and property disputes. The policy might provide cover against others, normally for contract disputes or debt recovery.

MARINE / AIR CARGO

Cover for goods being imported and exported. This form of cover can also include goods in transit to or from the place of manufacture, and to or from docks or airports.

MONEY COVER

Loss of cash and negotiable instruments such as cheques, post office and credit card vouchers, from your premises or whilst being transported there.

PRODUCT RECALL

If a manufacturer or supplier is compelled by law to recall a product from customers (normally due to a concern about a dangerous feature or the product's inability to meet government or EU regulations). This cover will pay the costs of the recall procedure and physical recovery of products.

PROFESSIONAL INDEMNITY

Financial losses suffered by your clients, where they allege it was because of negligence, errors, or omissions.

STOCK THROUGHPUT

This is a policy that combines marine or air cargo import and exports, along with stock in storage locations and domestic vehicle loads. It can incorporate deterioration of frozen food in cold stores and the trailers belonging to the haulier. This can be particularly useful for importers and hauliers with storage sites or distributions hubs. Throughput denotes goods on the move in all situations.

TRUSTEES' LIABILITY

As Directors' Liability but for the trustees on the boards of charities.

IN CONCLUSION

This is by no means an exhaustive list of the covers that can be arranged. There are many more for specific situations and the list of financial guarantees is almost endless. But the insurance classes above cover the majority of eventualities regularly insured in the UK.

Obviously, businesses won't require all of these covers, but the first six are almost universally purchased in one form or another. In a lot of cases they are packaged to form contracts for a specific purpose. New ones are being created all the time, especially for online sales. These include the following:

- Tradesman
- Property owners
- Shops

- Offices
- Hotels
- Restaurants
- Jewellers
- Sports clubs
- Marine/ air cargo
- Night clubs
- etc...

> ***Quick Tip***
>
> If you can find a packaged product that meets your requirements, then it is likely this will be the most cost-effective way to purchase business insurance. Packaged products are sold for simple situations, just make sure they do cover everything you intend to do.

It is almost unheard of nowadays for anyone to purchase Employers' Liability on its own and few insurers offer to do this, unless it is due to a very specific set of circumstances. Material damage and business interruption are the other core covers in any packaged product.

Finally, in regard to motor insurances, a lot of us grew up with Third Party Only (TPO), Third Party Fire & Theft (TPF&T) and Fully Comprehensive (COMP). Third party relates to damage or injury to other people and is required by law. It is included in Comprehensive cover.

With the rise of the claims culture and the increase in awards from the courts, especially for personal injuries, third party claims have become the most costly claim motor insurers deal with. Premiums have risen to reflect this and there is no longer any significant difference in cost between TPO, TPFT and COMP, unless the value of the vehicle is high. Most insurers only offer COMP.

8

YOUR ROUTE TO MARKET

In the UK you have two routes to market, they are:

Approach an insurer or scheme provider direct

or

engage with a broker who obtains terms for you.

THE DIRECT APPROACH FOR SMALL UK BUSINESSES

There are few insurers who deal direct with the public, unless it is for a product advertised online. Gone are the days you could walk into an insurer's office on the high street. If you do find them online you may recognise an insurer name such as AXA, Zurich, Allianz or Aviva, but sometimes you are dealing with a brand like More Than (which is actually Royal & Sun Alliance).

The brand you are dealing with will not be recognisable and may be one of the lesser-known insurers like Ageas, Covea or NIG, all substantial insurers as far as the industry is concerned.

You might even be dealing with a broker or scheme provider who is selling products backed by an insurer, but what they offer is limited to what they want to sell.

Maybe one shop policy, one office policy, or one property owner's policy. There is no independent comparative analysis of products from across the market, because they are only offering the ones they have arranged.

Good examples here are: Suttons who specialise in cleaning and security companies; Commercial Express, Towergate, and Simply Business. The cover (or capacity, as it is also known) will be provided by other insurers, perhaps those already mentioned, or others such as QBE, Hiscox, AIG, and certain syndicates at Lloyd's. At best these providers will give you a few insurers' quotes, but they will not have researched a wide range of insurers on your behalf.

VERY LARGE BUSINESSES

If you have a very large business and you can afford to employ risk managers and insurance professionals within your business, then you may be able to approach some insurers direct in London. The insurers you approach will expect to be dealing with professionals who understand the industry and have credible experience and qualifications.

You might save some money by employing this approach, but any savings may be lost in the wages you must pay. The real benefit here is in designing a bespoke solution and having the control firmly in your business. This may include large co-insurance provisions, first loss arrangements to limit total claims payments, and claims handling facilities dovetailed with your own insurance and legal departments.

If you can take a significant part of the

administration away from insurers and potentially limit losses by putting funds aside to meet some of them, you might be able to get substantial savings. This only tends to work on large scales where premiums are high.

PROS AND CONS

In any strategy there are always pros and cons. The secret is in getting the correct balance in a particular situation so that the advantages exceed the disadvantages. When buying your insurance direct you need to understand the factors, so you can analyse and weigh them correctly.

The main problems with the direct approach are:

- You have a seen a limited selection of contracts, even if you have spent hours searching and making surface-level comparisons.
- You have the illusion of a choice. In reality, you have been sold what was on offer at the time you looked. Just like going to the supermarket.
- You might assume that what you asked for is what you have purchased but what you get is what was available, even if it does not match your needs. What you have is the nearest equivalent and some cover may not be available.
- Your choice is not informed if you have no training in insurance. If you have no technical knowledge on which to base your decisions, your choice is based on the limited experience of buying insurance in the past. Did you read all the policy wording and did it make complete sense?

- As the industry changes if you are unaware of developments, in terms of cover, legal requirements or changes to products and policy wordings, do you have the best policy this time around?
- You might have been told the product is suitable for your situation, but it isn't independent advice, it's biased towards the provider's product. They will only discuss their own product and won't compare it to any other.
- Responsibility for suitability will fall squarely on your shoulders, not the insurer's.
- You won't have independent help if you need to make changes to cover.
- You won't receive independent help if you make a claim.
- When you get to the renewal date, you must start all over again if you want to make comparisons. The insurer isn't going to help.

Quick Tip

The perceived advantages in buying direct are that you will a) get the most competitive price, and b) find the cheapest by comparing several insurers. You might be lucky and get what you want, but if the price is too cheap it should set off alarm bells. Cheap premiums generally lead to stripped-down products. Look at the cover in detail, the excesses and restrictions in cover and make sure it really does meet your needs.

USING A BROKER

Using an independent professional broker has many benefits and very few downsides, *if* you pick the correct partner (discussed in the next section). You might pay a slightly higher price, but this is not necessarily the case. A serious commercial broker will have a wide range of insurers and contracts to choose from, almost none of which you will find online and this might lead to a cheaper premium.

Quick Tip

The best deal is almost never the cheapest. But the difference in price between the cheapest and the best might be only 10%. It is worth approaching an independent broker, even if you have found what you think is a good deal online. In this way you can compare product, process the service.

What can you expect from a professional broker and how will that benefit you?

- You should build a face to face relationship with an individual, who should visit you at your premises and will get to know you and your business in detail.
- They should be able to furnish you with information about their qualifications, professional accreditations, experience, and their ability to satisfy your needs.
- A good broker should explain the process, what they will do and how they will achieve the result you want. Everything should be open, honest, and transparent.
- They should be clear about how they will be remunerated, whether it's commission, a fee, or a combination and how they manage potential conflicts of interest.
- They should be clear about the insurers and markets they will approach, why they have selected them, and the result they expect.
- Once the broker has devised a solution for you, they should make a formal presentation to include:
    - Statements of facts
    - Policy schedules, including:
        - Covers provided
        - Sums insured
        - Limits of liability
        - Clauses
        - Conditions
        - Warranties

- Policy wordings
  - Insurance Product Information Documents (IPIDs)
  - Statements of demands and needs
  - Terms of business
  - Service Level Agreement (SLA)
  - Premium details including, tax and fees
  - Payment options

> ***Quick Tip***
>
> A broker might give you an indication of cost before providing information but they should never ask you to decide until you have had sufficient time to consider the proposed solution. This is called Contract Certainty and is an FCA rule.

You should be given an opportunity to ask questions about the proposed solution and should expect to get detailed answers so you can make an informed decision.

If the broker has not disclosed a fee and will be paid by a commission from the insurer(s), you are entitled to know how much this is. Only in this way can you determine whether the amount is reasonable in the circumstances. Ask, you are entitled to know.

If you decide to proceed with all or part of the solution, you should be furnished with confirmations of cover from the product providers, including all the relevant certificates you may need to provide to customers and authorities.

If you have chosen to use a premium financier proposed by the broker, then you should be given an agreement detailing the full terms and conditions of the finance. This is usually structured as a loan that you repay, whilst the capital amount is provided to the broker so they can pay the insurers on your behalf. The agreement can include any fees.

Thereafter the broker should give you full information about how they will deal with any mid-term adjustments you need to make, how they will deal with any claims that might arise, and how they will carry out the renewal review process.

Finally, you should expect your broker to contact you periodically to ensure your ongoing needs are being met and to provide you with information about evolving risks, new products and risk management services.

If you can find the right broker and build a professional relationship of trust, there really is no downside. You should get timely professional advice when you need it, ensuring your cover always matches the needs of your business as it evolves.

9

CHOOSING A BROKER

Brokers come in all shapes and sizes. It can be challenging knowing who will best meet your needs.

If all you need is a package policy to cover a single residential let property, an office, or a small shop, then most brokers who advertise business insurance should be able to deal with this for you. The products are generic, giving all the main covers you would expect with well-known insurance names such as Aviva, Zurich, or AXA.

If you have a business with your own risk managers and insurance trained staff, then you will most likely approach bigger brokers like AON, Marsh and Willis. If you're big enough, you may approach insurers direct.

Most business fall into neither of the two categories and need a solution that is more complex than a package, but they will not be big enough to engage an insurer or a global broker directly. These are the businesses that need to engage with an independent commercial broker.

Where to start? The internet is still a good place to start your search, but you should be clear about what you are looking for and which results you can discount immediately. If you search for business or commercial insurance brokers, you will get thousands of results from all over the UK. What you want is one with offices close enough who are happy to visit to get to know you and your business.

I would suggest you search for "commercial insurance brokers" followed by your locality. The nearest city or large town is good, as they probably contain one or two serious commercial brokers who will have the experienced, professional, commercial specialists you need.

> ***Quick Tip***
>
> If you have a recommendation from someone you trust in business and the broker is close enough to visit you, that's a good place to start.

The top few results are paid-for positions and if you follow them to their websites, they may not be local businesses. Below this you will often find a set of results with a map that is related to your search, these are likely to be what you're looking for. Always select the More Places button to reveal the full list of relevant commercial brokers.

If you scroll down in the list you should get at least twenty businesses with brief descriptions, with website links. High star ratings and testimonials are good ones to visit first.

You should immediately get a feel for the sort of business you are looking at and the type of work they do. They may be a national business with local offices or a regionally based business with clients in the area, or maybe further afield. All should be able to visit you to discuss your needs if you call them. If they can't come out to see you, deselect them and move on, unless you are based in a remote area.

You will also find more results on subsequent pages and some may be worth considering. Being on page two might indicate they aren't good at website design, not that they aren't good at insurance. However, the further you get from page one, the less relevant the results are likely to be.

The first thing you can do is look on the websites to see if there are specific references to your type of business. If they clearly focus on certain area of business and that matches yours they are likely to be a broker that can satisfy your needs. But, watch out for generic pages where only the profession is different – they are possibly playing search engines to get high rankings.

Make sure they are independent and able to approach more than one insurer, and are not tied to one. That said, if they are truly specialists in your area of business they are probably worth talking to. They may have policy wordings that are better than general cover.

HOW SHOULD YOU START YOUR CONVERSATION WITH A BROKER?

First, ask to speak to an experienced commercial broker. The response should be confident immediate and you should be put through to an individual who can deal with your enquiry. If there is delay or uncertainty, this is probably not a good sign.

Once through to the named individual, briefly explain your business and your requirements and ask if they can come out to visit you at your premises.

If the broker is a professional, they will jump at the

chance to get to know you and see what you do, where you do it, and how. It is essential they understand your business, to get you the best possible deal.

If they do not want to come out or are hesitant, make your excuses and say goodbye. Put the phone down and strike them off the list.

If they engage positively, you should ask some critical questions.

Are they independent?

The answer should be YES. Completely independent to place business where they like, with no direction from any other organisation, and working only for the benefit of the customer, you.

Are they directly regulated?

Again, the answer should be YES. If they are an appointed representative of another organisation, why? Do they accept direction by the parent body?

How many insurers do they hold agencies with?

If they only have a few agencies, then their access to markets will be severely limited and they may not find you the best deal.

Do they have experience of businesses in your sector?

Self-evident, if they do, they have a head start on understanding what you do and which insurers might satisfy your needs. If they don't, they must start from scratch and it might take longer to put together a solution.

Do they have examples of businesses you know?

If they say yes, ask for a name you can check. Common sense.

Which insurers would they consider approaching?

If they have experience, they will have a good idea who they will approach.

Do they place business in the London Market?

This is a credibility check. If they don't you should question their credibility as a serious commercial broker. There are always situations that need this facility and without it they would struggle to place some risks.

How long will it take to provide a recommendation?

You can't hang around, you need a solution, unless you're really prepared and searching well in advance of your renewal. As a guide:

- Single premises depending on complexity of processes or high-risk hazards – 1-2 weeks.
- Multiple premises requiring site visits, with an easily understandable operation – 2-6 weeks.
- Large businesses with complex operations, multiple operational models – 6-12 weeks.

How long have they been in the industry?

Insurance is about trust and credibility between brokers and underwriters. The longer a broker has been in the industry, the more likely they will be able to deliver.

How are they remunerated – commission or fees?

This deserves further examination.

> ***Quick Tip***
> A broker isn't obliged to tell you how much their commission is, unless you ask, then they are obliged to under FCA rules. If they say they don't know it's a fib, everyone knows what their margins are. If they are vague it's a good reason to be cautious; push them to confirm the amount - you might be shocked.

COMMISSION

If a broker is remunerated by commission, there are three potential issues.

First there is a potential conflict of interest, in that the broker may place the business where they get the most commission, regardless of whether other policies might provide better cover.

Second, as commission is part of the premium you will pay tax on that element, which increases the total premium.

Third, you have no idea whether the broker's earnings are reasonable for the work they have done, and will do to maintain the policy throughout the year.

Commissions range from 10% on motor business, 25% is normal on combined property and liability, up to a whacking 40% on residential and commercial property business. This will depend on the size of the broker and their insurer relationships.

FEES

If the broker is remunerated by fees, then it's simpler. No commission, no conflict of interest, and the broker won't care how cheap the insurance is, as their earnings have nothing to do with the premium. In fact, they will actively seek out the cheapest for you, as they are more likely to get your business.

As there is no tax on professional fees in insurance, you will immediately save 12% (at time of going to press) on the broker's earnings and this reduces the total cost.

Under FCA regulations, fees must be disclosed up front, in writing, before the client decides to proceed. This means you get to see what the broker is earning and you can decide whether it is reasonable. You might even be able to negotiate the fee. It's open, honest and transparent.

Now you've asked a few searching questions, the responses should give you a feeling about the individual and business. It's essential you feel comfortable with that person, you will develop a relationship of trust and you can't do that if you don't like or trust the individual or their business.

HOW MANY BROKERS TO USE?

Now this is probably one of the most important parts of the entire exercise. How many brokers will you actively engage to prepare terms for you? One, two, three, or more?

If you have found what you believe to be serious commercial brokerages, who are independent, with multiple agencies, then the answer to this is two at most and no more. That said, if you find one with whom you feel very comfortable and who you are sure will do the job, and everything they have said and done appears credible, intelligent, open and honest, then you may be happy to work with them alone.

But surely more brokers means more chance of finding the cheapest and best solution? This is where industry knowledge is critical – you couldn't be more wrong. Let me explain:

Every decent commercial broker will deal with a range of insurers and there will be a good deal of overlap. They should all be dealing with the big five; Allianz, Aviva, AXA, RSA, and Zurich. There's a good chance the majority will all have agencies with likes of NIG, Ageas, Covea and others in niche or specialist markets.

The critical issue is to ensure that your presentation is seen by each insurer only once and you need to be in control of this. You need to know who the brokers are approaching and limit their activity. If you choose too many brokers, it is almost impossible to remain in control.

Why would this be?

If a busy underwriter sees your presentation from more than one broker, they are likely to think it is being touted around the market to put pressure on the current insurer. They will think there is little chance of getting the business and time spent on preparing terms would be better expended on a piece of business they are more confident of securing. They will decline the quote and move on to something else. Remember, they have limited time and lots of quotes to look at. Time is most definitely money and they don't waste it.

If an insurer only sees a proposal once, they assume there is a chance of getting the business. They are therefore more likely to seriously discuss it with the broker.

> ***Quick Tip***
>
> Limit the number of brokers you work with. Trying to play one off against another on price will backfire as you'll find it harder to get competitive quotes.

How do we ensure each insurer only sees it once?

First, we limit the numbers of brokers we approach so the chances of it hitting the same insurer twice is low. Two is ideal.

Whether the first broker is your existing one or not ask them who they will approach. Ask for the names of the insurers and tell them you intend to ask one more broker to look at your business, for comparison, and that you will tell them not to approach the named insurers. Don't accept more than five names. Any more is unreasonable and they may just be giving you a list to stop another broker going there. They might be looking to block markets. More of this later.

You then tell broker two who the first broker has approached, and that they are not to approach them, but that they are free to approach others. In this way, no insurer should see the business more than once and all will feel they have a good chance of securing the business and put in serious effort.

Finally, you tell both brokers that if you find out they

have approached insurers outside those they originally disclosed, you will not be placing business with them, ever. If they feel later they should approach another insurer, they should come back to you first to check whether it has already been covered or not. You don't want any insurer to see your business twice.

If you engage three or more brokers the chances of you keeping control are lost. At some point there will be an overlap, an underwriter will see it more than once. Even if the other broker is in another part of the country, it will be logged on a central system and they will obviously decline to quote against themselves. The first thing an underwriter does when presented with a risk is to check if it has been seen somewhere else in their business.

Professional brokers will respect your knowledge and it will make you more credible in their eyes. They know you are serious and you know what you are doing, so they don't have to pussyfoot around you. It also means they know that if they come up with the best terms, they have a great chance of securing your business and that makes professionals work harder.

BLOCKING MARKETS

Less professional brokers will seek to block markets; to prevent other brokers from getting quotes. If an insurer gets a presentation from a broker, then in most cases they will not give a quote to another broker until they have given the terms to the first one and then they will only give the same terms. In this way the insurer only puts one quote into the market for that case and once the first broker is logged on their central system, this can't be overridden.

How does that block markets? A broker seeking to defend their business or increase their chance of getting a piece of business will use a shotgun approach and send their presentation to as many insurers as they have email addresses. They will seek to get their name logged before anyone else has a chance and thus prevent another broker getting terms.

The blocking broker does not intend to have detailed conversations with all insurers. It is likely that he has a preferred insurer in mind, very often it will be the one paying the highest commission. They will not pursue detailed terms or quotes from those insurers, they simply want to block other brokers from getting terms which might be better than the ones they will put forward. At best its lazy, and at worst its downright dishonest. It's *always* unprofessional. If the proposal doesn't win on its merits, then the broker should not seek to prevent the client from obtaining a better solution.

How would you find out? Other brokers will tell you another broker has already been there. If it happens you know what's going on. If you find a broker doing it, ditch them straight away – they don't have your best interests at heart.

WORKING TOGETHER

It's a partnership, not a fight. A professional broker wants to do their very best for you because they want to satisfy your needs and, of course, win your business. The cheaper the solution is, the more likely it is that they will get your business, so they don't really want to inflate the premium to make a few extra quid in commission. It isn't worth the risk of failing to get your business. They are more likely to go in low with a reasonable earning and not take chances. Remember, brokers want your recurring business, not just one year.

Your part in this partnership is to tell them everything they want to know. The more information you give, the more likely they will convince an insurer to lower the premium. If you really want to achieve a good result then enter into the broker partnership in a fully engaging manner.

If they ask you a question it's because they need the answer. Holding back information makes it difficult to get the best cover.

This includes telling them what your target premium is. Some clients don't want to say because they fear a quote just a bit less than they are paying already. It's very difficult to hit a target if they don't know what it is. In addition, if they can't tell an insurer what the target is, they may question your credibility. That leads to no quote.

If you choose a fee-based brokerage, the conflict is removed, you can disclose fully and sit back and wait for a presentation with a competitive premium.

Get ready before the meeting, it means it will move quicker and waste less of your time, and your broker is less likely to come back to you for additional information.

10

PREPARING INFORMATION

Insurance is about risk and uncertainty. The higher the level of uncertainty in the insurer's mind, the higher the premium. You must help the insurer understand your business and the risks inherent in it.

> ***Quick Tip***
>
> There is one key thing to understand – information is power. The more you can present to an insurer the lower the premium is likely to be.

What information do you need to prepare? Detailed information about every aspect of your business activity.

- A business plan is always good if you have one.
- Annual turnover – total invoices.
- Gross profit – turnover less cost of sales (no more).
- Wages split by; Directors, clerical and managerial, manual workers.
- How much you work away from premises.
- Do you work at height or in other hazardous situations?

- Contract values.
- Hired-in plant costs.
- Sums insured for buildings, equipment, stock
- Business policies, procedures, and method statements detailing how you do what you do and the controls around completion of your work.
- Health and Safety policy, or if you have fewer than five staff risk assessments for the main activities you undertake.
- Quality HR documents, including staff contracts, staff handbook

You need to convince the insurer you are firmly in control of your business and are unlikely to let any risks go unnoticed.

If you have a management controls framework for any regulatory authority you deal with, it serves the same purpose as the above.

Details of any quality accreditations you have are always good as they speak highly of your business. ISO and industry standards, Chartered status are all good things to disclose. The higher the quality of your operation, the lower the premium will be.

If you have high value premises their construction is important. Things that burn well, like wood or composite foam panels will be negative factors.

Security is important if you have lots of attractive equipment or stock. A bells-only alarm is the minimum, as are five-lever mortice deadlocks on all entry and exit doors and key-operated window locks. A system that signals to a twenty-four-hour monitoring station will almost certainly be required and will bring premium reductions.

In all cases a copy of your standard Terms of Business or Client Contract is essential. A well-written set of terms of business defines rights and responsibilities, and governs the relationship between you and your customer. To the extent responsibilities are defined, it will limit your liability to the client which all feeds in to an insurer being able to defend you in the event of a claim.

Leaflets, brochures, promotional documents, and your website are also sources of information that will help an insurer to quantify risks. A note of caution here. If there is content on your website that makes you look like a bigger business and that you offer services you've never actually performed (and probably never will) make sure the broker or insurer knows so it can be discounted, especially if it looks hazardous or dangerous.

If you are a professional providing advice of any kind and want Professional Indemnity cover, then your insurer is going to want to see the CVs of all consultants giving advice. A CV will allow them to get a feel for qualifications and experience. A good CV will lead to lower premiums.

You will also be asked about your claims experience. If your business has been running for some time, you will need to prepare a list of all claims in the last five years, including an explanation of each event, what you have done since to ensure it doesn't happen again, and the costs involved. You should also include any events that might have given rise to a claim, most importantly anything of which you are currently aware. There is a central claims register and if you fail to disclose something important, it could lead to your policy being cancelled *ab initio* (from the beginning) as if it never happened. Any open claims would be closed without payment. This could include sizeable claims against you.

You will also be asked about any previous businesses that went into liquidation, administration, or bankruptcy. If any of these occurred to you personally or in a business in which you were a director, then you need a good explanation as to what happened and why.

Finally, if you have ever been convicted of any non-motoring offences, these must be divulged if they are still within their disclosure period.

Remember, failure to disclose information within your knowledge will lead to claims being refused or the cover being cancelled. That means loss of premium, no claim, and perhaps extensive damages to pay. It may be embarrassing, but the consequences of non-disclosure will be far worse.

Whilst the Insurance Act 2015 lays a heavier burden on your broker to ask you the right questions, that does not absolve you from failing to mention something you know is relevant. The relationship between broker, client and insurer is based on the principal of *uberrima fides* (utmost good faith). It is this principle that means each party must be open, honest, and give a full account of everything they know.

11

THE NEW-BUSINESS PROCESS

You have met your broker(s) and they have conducted a detailed fact find with you. You didn't hold anything back and they have as much information as they need to put together a comprehensive presentation to insurers.

If they are smart they will have taken photographs to send to underwriters. A picture speaks a thousand words. Try to explain something in text and an underwriter may or may not understand, but if I show them a picture, often the response will be, "Oh yeah, I know what that is." Remember, we want to remove uncertainty in the mind of the underwriter. Let your broker take pictures if they want to.

In addition, broker(s) should have taken copies of documents and marketing materials, as laid out in the previous chapter.

Now you wait. Every quote done properly takes a time and your broker should give you a good idea how long the process will take. A month is reasonable (unless the risk is simple) to prepare a detailed presentation and have enough time to approach insurers. More time equals more markets.

Your broker should come back to you with a report of their activity. This might include how far negotiations have gone, with which insurers, and what are their initial feelings. At this point they might ask for some additional information underwriters have requested, if they do, provide it.

Once the broker has presented the risk to insurers they should be able to recommend to you the company that comes up with the best terms, conditions, and price. They won't feed this price back to the insurer's competitors to drive the price down. If they have done their job correctly, they don't need to; it should already be the best policy. Remember, they need to maintain long-term relationships and horse-trading on every quote isn't the way to achieve that.

THE QUOTE

You should receive their final recommendations. Because of FCA regulations these are in a prescribed format, covering everything you need to know to make an informed decision. This is called Contract Certainty, and it must be fulfilled before you can be expected to make a decision.

> ***Quick Tip***
>
> Your broker might tell you what price they have arrived at over the phone, to see if it is satisfactory, but they should never ask you to make a decision until they have presented the terms.

What should the presentation include? For a policy of insurance to be "Contract Certain" several documents must be provided. If these have not been provided the policy is not contract certain and the client can under certain circumstances walk away from the contract.

COVERING LETTER

This typically sets out everything about the brokerage, including regulation, quote terms, additional cover offers, the price, instalment facilities, and how they will service clients.

STATEMENT OF DEMANDS AND NEEDS (THE IMPORTANT INFORMATION DOCUMENT)

This sets out:

- What you requested
- The basis of recommendation
- Significant factors about the terms presented
- Things you asked for, which could not be provided

STATEMENT OF FACTS

This feeds back all the information presented to insurers, so the customer can check it is correct and accurate and can challenge it before going on cover.

SCHEDULE OF COVER

This is the most important document. It sets out the specific sections of cover provided, the sums insured, limits of indemnity, and the extent of cover provided. It sets out any specific conditions that apply. These could include a security requirement or height limit, for example.

INSURER PRODUCT INFORMATION DOCUMENT (IPID)

This was called the Key Facts or Summary of Product Cover, but every insurer's document was different. Some were better than others. In the most recent EU Insurance Distribution Directive, a set format was approved so all insurers' documents follow the same template.

Insurance Conduct of Business Rules (ICOBS) state that this format must be followed exactly for personal insurances. For commercial insurance there may be some variation to layout, but the information requested is the same.

FULL POLICY WORDING

This is the full policy wording, which includes the detail for every section of the policy, even those sections that have not been chosen by the client:

- Definition of terms
- Regulatory information
- Claims information and helplines
- How to make a complaint
- Section wordings and exclusions
- General conditions applying to the whole policy
- General exclusions applying to the whole policy
- Identity of the insurers

BROKER TERMS OF BUSINESS

This is the document which outlines the relationship between broker and client. It sets out what the client can expect, how the broker is regulated and remunerated, and the client's responsibilities. It includes information relating to mid-term alterations, claims, security of insurers, documentation and payment of premiums, handling of client money, confidentiality, and the FCA Compensation Scheme.

SUMMARY

This is really the minimum that should be provided, although the broker may provide additional information about their business, additional products and services they could arrange or make introductions for.

If a broker is offering additional services or is introducing you to another business, then you should ask about the additional income the broker will receive.

Once the quote has been provided, a reasonable amount of time should be allowed to read and consider the information and ask questions, raise concerns, or challenge inaccuracies. Twenty-four hours should be allowed as a minimum and under no circumstances should the broker send the information by email and then call the client for an immediate decision. That is not treating the customer fairly.

If terms cannot be provided until the last minute, which is not ideal, but occasionally unavoidable, the client can instruct cover, subject to making alterations after the event.

NEGOTIATIONS

It is at this point that the client can question the broker over their commission and fees. If no fee is disclosed, then it is a certainty that the broker is being remunerated by commission from the insurer. Whilst the broker is not obliged to volunteer this information up front, if you ask they **must** tell you immediately. Fees must be disclosed up front, so you should see them within the financial details section of the broker's quote letter.

Once you have questioned the broker about their earnings, you will be able to make the judgement of whether they appear reasonable in the circumstances. You can ask the broker to prepare a detailed costing of services.

> ***Quick Tip***
>
> Some brokers add fees on top of commission. If you are paying a fee, ask if there is commission too.

If you think the overall earnings are too high, you are within your rights to negotiate fees and commissions.

The earnings should not be a percentage of the price, they should reflect the amount of work the broker will be expected to do throughout the year. In a detailed costing the hours of work should reflect the personnel who will conduct the work.

If you can come to an agreement about the overall price, including the broker's earnings and the scope of cover provided, you can move on to the next stage.

INSTRUCTIONS

Once you are happy with the quote terms and have had an opportunity to make amendments and alterations, the broker will expect to get instructions from you to proceed. This can be done verbally, but more normally by email, including the method of payment.

The broker will convey these instructions to the insurer and ask them to go on cover including a start date. If motor cover is arranged a cover note or certificate should be issued immediately (essential for taxing a vehicle).

> ***Quick Tip***
> Make sure your broker sends you a confirmation of cover by email, so you have something to rely on before policy documentation arrives. You never know when a loss may occur.

Under FCA regulations insurers are required to provide full policy documentation within thirty days. In most cases, digital systems provide PDF documents within twenty-four hours, including the Employers' Liability certificate. The more complex the solution, the longer documents take to prepare. Seven working days is usually more than enough. Chase if they haven't arrived by then.

If the client has not done so already, they must provide their PAYE reference number, to comply with the Employers' Liability Tracing Office regulations, if this cover is part of the policy. PAYE Ref – (Known as the ERN Employers Reference Number) will be in a specific format: 075 / RA50749

If this is not provided within thirty days, the insured party will come off cover.

The premium must be paid immediately as cover is effective immediately. The alternative is to pay by instalment by completing an agreement so that funds can be released to pay the insurers. The client repays the loan over ten or twelve months, or they pay the insurers direct on their own agreement. Direct debit agreements should be signed immediately, often by email and electronic signature.

12

ONGOING SERVICES & RENEWALS

MID-TERM ADJUSTMENTS (MTAs)

Once on cover you must communicate alterations, amendments, or changes in activities immediately, so the broker can give you advice and act on your instructions and ensure that cover remains in force and accurate.

The broker will be led by your demands and needs. They cannot be expected to read your mind and recommend complete cover without information, direction, and evidence of a requirement, or a request for cover.

In respect of motor insurances, alterations must be communicated immediately. Either the insurer or the broker must update the Motor Insurers Database (MID). This is the online record able to be searched by the police to identify vehicles covered under UK insurances, including who is allowed to drive them. If you don't communicate a vehicle change immediately, you risk seizure of the vehicle by the police and a fine and points for having no valid insurance.

ADVICE AND GUIDANCE

One of the most important and valuable reasons for using a broker is to gain access to professional advice. No broker is going to tell you how to do your job or how to run your business, but what they can do is advise you on the implications and or consequences of your plans. This advice can include:

- Risk management
- Health and safety
- Security
- Construction
- Fire alarms
- Sprinkler systems
- Legal liability
- Employees
- HR issues
- Business interruption
- Product recall
- Credit risk
- Professional liability
- Import / export
- Disaster management
- Business continuity planning
- Driver training and education
- International exposure
- ...and more...

The advice you can receive is considerable, but this will depend on the individual you deal with, their length of service in the industry, and the experience and qualifications they have. It will also depend on the type of businesses they have dealt with.

A lot of this will be free at the point of request and will only be chargeable if you ask the broker to undertake a considerable piece of work on your behalf. An example of this might be the construction and delivery of a Business Continuity Plan or a Driver's Handbook and Safety Policy.

This advice can save considerable amounts of money. In one case over £20,000 was saved by telling a client what they didn't need to do; when constructing a mezzanine storage area in a large factory. They intended to extend the sprinkler system into an area where it wasn't required by insurers. It was simple, effective, cost-saving advice.

CLAIMS MANAGEMENT

Sometimes clients have a poor claims record. This often evidences itself on fleet policies in terms of employee injuries. The claims result from poor health and safety regimes or lack of training. Sometimes repeated claims can be traced directly to a defective process, policy, practice, product or individual employee or manager. Whilst claims rise, premiums will never decrease, so there is an advantage to the insured in working to reduce claims.

It is often the case that the insured is too close to the day-to-day business or lacks the skills and expertise to stand back and see what's going wrong. Good commercial brokers can almost sense what is happening, just by looking at the operation and analysing the activities of the business.

Sometimes the cause is obvious, and sometimes it requires a deeper understanding of the business and exactly how they operate.

In one case a poor fleet claims record was eventually tracked back to driver fatigue, which then led to poor decisions, which at the outset just looked like careless behaviour. Steps were simple and effective.

Speed limiters were taken of vehicles so they could drive at 70 mph on the motorway and were not restricted to 50 mph. This meant jobs were completed faster and drivers were at the wheel for shorter periods of time.

Cameras and GPS tracking were introduced so a detailed analysis could be done on driving performance and this led to improved driver training. It also meant drivers knew that a spotlight was on their driving and they became more careful.

Finally, it was discovered that some drivers were doing three-day jobs, in two days and taking a day off. The only way they could do this was by starting ridiculously early, 5:00 am was not unusual, and finishing late, around 10:00 pm. They were doing seventeen-hour days. These were small flatbed vehicles, so they did not have or need tachometers. Managers had never known this was going on; drivers never told them.

Employee injuries can be costly and whilst these claims persist premiums continue to rise. Engaging with your broker and health and safety consultants can have a significant effect on claims and therefore premiums.

Lots of small claims, and multiple claims from the same individuals can signal bad practice. A claims culture can even arise where employees see minor injuries as a payout from the employer's insurer, at little personal risk to themselves. This is immediately apparent from the claims history. It comes down to lax procedures and a lack of oversight by operational managers. When professional managers control activity there are far fewer events leading to injuries. If employees are found to be complicit in fraud, tight control and oversight can identify and eliminate it.

When external consultants are required, a broker can be instrumental in recommending professionals who can help the client in specific areas of their business. This approach saves the client employing multiple consultants. In this way the client can rely on effective professionals with whom the broker has worked over many years. It should also ensure that what they do will be beneficial and acceptable to the insurers, and by using properly qualified consultants will also mean that the charges they make will be reasonable.

13

CLAIMS

Probably the most important part of any brokers service, is how they deal with claims, as it is only when a claim arises that you find out if what you paid was worth the price.

Regardless of what the situation is, you should have immediate access to an experienced claims manager who should take ownership of the situation and be prepared to help you do whatever is needed to conclude the claim as quickly as possible.

If your broker gives you a number to call and leaves you to the insurer's service they have failed in their professional duty. You need advice to prepare and communicate the claim, how to report it and the broker should collect the information from you and report it themselves. If the insurer requires information the broker should co-ordinate and make sure it goes to the insurer in the correct format.

BUSINESS INTERRUPTION

If there is a claim to be made for a loss of income following a material damage claim, the broker may have arranged cover to pay the costs of a professional loss adjustor who will act for you. Lorega provide such a service, which gives immediate advice and assistance and will provide full hands-on management of the damage and business interruption claim.

With this service you can get on with rebuilding your business, whilst the loss adjustor working for you will deal with every aspect of the claim. It often means that the claim concludes faster too. You are not left with lots of work to prepare the claim for the insurer, when you don't really know what they want or how they want it presented. The loss adjustor may also be able to negotiate a quick advance payment on day one. The broker will be able to co-ordinate this work.

DAMAGE TO PROPERTY

If the claim is for damage or loss to property, then the broker may have access to contractors who can carry out emergency work and reinstate damage to an acceptable standard. It pays to use broker relations as they will have been tested over time and should be reliable. The costs should also be acceptable to the loss adjustor working for the insurer.

LIABILITY CLAIMS

If the claim relates to a liability and your insurers are looking to amass information so they can defend you, then the broker is likely to be present when the insurer conducts a liability investigation. The broker should brief you on what to expect and lead you through the insurer's visit, helping you to give them the information they need.

The insurer's lawyers will then take over and deal directly with the claimant.

MOTOR INSURANCES

When a motor claim is reported the broker will arrange a repair with the insurer's recommended repairers and a courtesy vehicle whilst the vehicle is being repaired. If the claim was the fault of another road user, the broker should be able to deal with uninsured loses, such as the excess, hiring charges and the repair if you only have Third Party Fire & Theft. If there are personal injuries the broker should also be able to arrange for legal services to reclaim the cost of damages for the injured person(s).

In all cases, regardless of the claim type, the broker should lead the client through the claim to a successful conclusion and keep them informed throughout.

14

INSTALMENT FACILITIES

There are three ways customers can pay their premiums by instalments:

- The insurer's agreement
- The broker's agreement
- A premium financier's agreement

INSURER AGREEMENTS

These agreements are linked directly to the insurance policy, so if the customer fails to make a payment, after due enquiry the insurer can cancel the policy. The broker is not responsible for payment of the premium, responsibility remains squarely with the customer. Credit checks are conducted.

Generally, such agreements run for twelve months (the term of the policy) and a deposit is often required in the first twelve months, typically 20%. Interest rates vary, but are typically between 6-8% per annum. The agreement will then run continually from year to year, as long as the customer remains with that insurer.

BROKER AGREEMENTS

Under these arrangements the agreement is not linked directly to the insurance policy. The broker is responsible for payment of the premium to the insurer and uses its own funds to do this. The client then repays the broker including an interest charge. The broker retains the right to cancel the policy in the event of default and recover a return of premium to offset the balance due on the loan.

Generally, these agreements run for ten months, so any return premium is larger than the amount outstanding on the loan. A deposit is often required in the first twelve months, maybe as little as 10%. Interest rates vary, but are generally lower than those charged by insurers, making them more attractive to customers.

The premium will run continually from year to year and, even if the insurer changes, the new premium is simply applied to the new agreement each year.

PREMIUM FINANCIERS

These are finance companies that provide commercial funds to clients so they can spread their payments over the period of the insurance contract. Brokers normally partner with one or two providers such as Premium Credit Limited or Close Brothers. There are several other smaller companies. Credit checks are conducted.

The finance provider retains the right to instruct the broker to cancel the insurance in the event of a default. The return premium is then used to offset the amount outstanding on the loan. If the return of premium is not enough to pay off the loan, the financier will contact the customer to repay any outstanding balance.

Agreements can run for ten or twelve months, so any return premium is larger than the amount outstanding on the loan. Deposits are sometimes required and interest rates are lower than those charged by insurers.

The premium will run continually from year to year and, even if the insurer changes, the new premium is simply applied to the new agreement each year.

15

PERSONAL INSURANCES

Whether you are the principal in an unincorporated business, a director in a limited company, or a self-employed contractor, you are going to need to arrange personal insurances.

With the advent of direct insurers this market has changed out of all recognition. Some of the cheapest prices are found online, but you should still think about how you purchase them. There are five basic categories:

- Household Buildings, Contents and All-Risk for Portable Possessions and Valuables
- Private Car Insurances and Small Commercial Vehicles
- Travel
- Caravans
- Pet Insurance

THE HIGH STREET

There are still a lot of high street brokers, both independent and national chains. In most cases you can buy insurance over the counter and face to face with an individual who will take all your circumstances into account and look at several insurers before making a recommendation. They will have computer systems that allow them to source quotes from a range of insurers, finding the most appropriate products for you at a competitive price.

If you deal with a high street broker in this way you will get advice about suitability, help when you need to make changes, and help when you make a claim. This may suit you if you have a local broker. It does allow you to build up a relationship over time with individuals you can trust.

If you need specialist cover on a high net worth basis for antiques or valuable possessions, or if you have a property valued at over £1,000,000, or contents over £100,000, you need specialist advice. Buying online is not sensible and is highly likely to leave you exposed to risk.

This also applies if you need family fleet insurance. If you have several expensive vehicles, or cars used by your children as well as yourself, a family fleet can be a good option. Range Rovers, supercars and Bentleys fall into this category, but most policies insist on a first vehicle with a value over £35,000. A typical family fleet has 3-5 vehicles.

Some national chains, such as Swinton's, do not give comparative quotes and only offer a range of products they have arranged with single insurers, so remember this when buying your insurance from them. Ask the question about independence and whole of market or limited access to insurers.

Whilst you will get a more personal service dealing with an individual on the high street, it will probably cost you a little more than dealing direct or online. Services of this kind can be worth their weight in gold when you need it. There is no possibility of falling for an online scam or a ghost broker.

ONLINE AND DIRECT

When you buy online, you give your details to the insurer via a portal. You may use a comparison site, but we will start with a single insurer. Even if you use an aggregator's comparison site, you will inevitably have to conclude the contract with one insurer.

Insurers dealing direct with the public (e.g. Direct Line, Admiral, Hastings, Elephant, etc) make some of their money out of car insurance, but a lot is made from additional services such as: legal services for personal injury and uninsured losses; credit repair; hire; operation of repair facilities; financing; and the interest they earn on a very large pot of money. Even in times of low interest rates, if the pot is large interest can be considerable.

That doesn't mean the insurers don't care about you as a customer, but they do want to keep you happy so you continue to contribute to their pot. The service must be good or you will spend your money elsewhere, but be under no illusion your individual circumstances are largely irrelevant, other than they need them to issue documents.

The premium you pay in the first year is often cheap, and you'll probably choose one of the cheapest that's available. That's because you search a *price* comparison site, not a *cover* comparison site. This gets you to make your first contribution to the insurer's coffers. Along the way they will make offers for things like hire cars, breakdown, and other insurance policies – emergency home cover, alarms, travel insurance, and more. Some are now moving into utilities. These are ways of getting you to make ever-larger contributions to their pot.

> Quick Tip
>
> Car and house insurance are a licence to print money. Consider this as a commodity. It could be oil, orange juice or coffee. You must negotiate, rather than expect a reduction in premium resulting from your clean insurance record or the details you give.

When you renew your insurance, even though you may have made no claims, the premium is likely to be far greater than you originally paid. This is the insurer trying to get you to make a larger contribution. If you pay without thinking or let an instalment agreement continue, they've just scored a win. If you question it you will probably be told its normal rates and the first premium was an introductory offer. Never fall for that. Simply go elsewhere and get another introductory offer.

But there are more subtle ways to negotiate. If you approach them early, the figure will be high and they are unlikely to move on it, there is still plenty of time so they hold out for the larger figure. If you go back closer to the renewal date, when there is little time for them to secure your contribution, you should be able to get a lower price. After all, they don't want to lose your annual contribution and something is better than nothing.

Look around for quotes and always say you have a figure from an alternate insurer and make sure the figure you quote is about £50 less than you want. The direct insurer will almost always quote about £35-40 more than the figure you give them. They are hoping you can't be bothered to go back to another insurer and start again. In this way you should get the price you want.

Finally, ask for add-ons. Remember, they don't really care what they give you. They want a larger contribution to their pot, so if you pay a bit more, make sure you get something for it. Legal expenses, bonus protection, breakdown, courtesy vehicle, and family travel cover are examples of what you might get… if you ask.

HOUSEHOLD BUILDINGS & CONTENTS INSURANCE

This is a simple contract that covers the majority of things that can go wrong in or to your house. Standard cover includes:

- Fire
- Lightning
- Explosion
- Subsidence (the ground under property dropping away)
- Ground heave (the ground under property rising up)
- Landslip (ground moving downhill on a slope)
- Theft
- Malicious damage (vandalism or mindless damage with malicious intent)

- Impact (vehicles or animals hitting a building at speed)
- Aerials
- Riot
- Storm
- Flood
- Burst pipes
- Pedal cycles (accidental damage or theft)
- Personal money (cash carried or in the home and misused credit cards)
- Frozen food (deterioration after failure of the electric supply)
- Accidental damage

These are standard perils, apart from accidental damage, which is normally an optional extra.

> ***Quick Tip***
> Always take accidental damage on buildings and contents. The biggest cause of claims after burst pipes is other accidental damage. Things get dropped and knocked over all the time.

Under standard contents cover a limit of £2,500 normally applies for any one item or set, so if you have expensive furniture, antiques or works of art, make sure your insurers know, even if they never leave the house. Take pictures and get valuations. On most policies the maximum allowed for all valuables is 25-33% of the sum insured. If you have a lot of valuables, then you need to increase the basic sum insured so it is three or four times the valuables amount. Check with your insurer on the actual limit if you are unsure.

You will also want cover for valuable and portable possessions away from the home. This is called the All-Risks section, Unspecified and Specified. It is so-named because in addition to accidental damage cover; it includes cover for pure loss. On some polices you only get cover for pedal cycles, money, misuse of credit cards and frozen food when you take All-Risks cover.

Under the unspecified section you state an amount equivalent to the maximum amount of goods you might have away from your home at any one time. What you take on holiday as a family is a good start. Remember to add in all the jewellery, tablets, laptops, phones, cameras, cash, and clothes.

The unspecified section normally limits any one item to around £1,500, but this varies. Always know what your single article limit is as you will need to specify any items that exceed this limit. It is normally engagement rings and expensive watches. The limit for pedal cycles is normally £250, so one worth more than this must be specified, along with sets of golf clubs (which are considered one item), earrings, and other pairs or sets.

You may also be offered things like extra cover for contents in the open – shrubs and flowers in the garden, home emergency breakdowns, and guttering. Be clear what you need, what is covered, and what is not.

CARS & SMALL COMMERCIAL VEHICLES

These both come in three versions:

- Third Party Only (damage to other people only)
- Third Party Fire and theft, as before plus fire and theft
- Comprehensive which includes accidental damage to your own vehicle.

Classes of use for private cars are:

- Social, domestic and pleasure
- Plus, commuting to and from work
- Plus, personal business use – Class 1 (This only works if you are self-employed)
- Plus, use of your employer or partner – Class 2 (most businesses including Limited Companies)
- Plus, commercial travelling – Class 3 (e.g. sales reps)

Obviously, you start at the top and stop adding uses once you have the use you need. The further down you go the more expensive it becomes. Class 2 adds about 25% to Class 1 and Class 3 adds about 30% to Class 2.

For commercial vehicles it is different:

- Social domestic and pleasure plus business of the insured (normal for all business)
- Plus, carriage of own goods
- Plus, carriage of goods for hire or reward (hauliers/couriers carrying goods for others)

DESCRIPTIONS OF VEHICLES

On private car policies this will be the registration number and this vehicle has full cover under the policy. The policy often gives emergency third party cover to drive other vehicles. This does **not** cover damage to the vehicle, just the legal right to be on the road, and damage or injury to other people.

On a commercial vehicle or a fleet policy the registration number will be specified or, on larger fleets, it will say, "Any motor vehicle owned by the Insured." Even when this is the case changes must be notified immediately so the Motor Insurance Database can be amended.

Commercial vehicle policies rarely give cover to the named driver for any other vehicles unless the description is "Any motor vehicle in the care, custody or control of the Insured."

The exception is policies designed for the motor trade.

PERSONS ENTITLED TO DRIVE

On private car policies it will be one of:

- Insured only
- Insured and spouse
- Insured and named drivers
- Any authorised driver

On commercial vehicle policies it could be one of:

- Insured only (if it's an individual)
- Named drivers
- Any driver over twenty-five
- Any driver over thirty
- Any authorised driver

> ***Quick Tip***
> If you are looking at restricting the policy to named drivers to save money, if any are under twenty-five or there are more than four, you will be paying the same rate as any driver, so you may as well go for that level. Below that you will normally get discounts. Having a female on your policy, if you're male, will often get you a discount.

On a fleet policy or any policy in the name of a company it will always be "any authorised driver" but the premium may be rated on drivers over a certain age, although it will not say this on the certificate. It will be stated on the schedule of cover.

OTHER PERSONAL INSURANCES

There are many other personal insurance including cover for pets, caravans and travel. If you have not already got them along with house or motor insurance, then you should look online for the cheapest version available from a reputable company. You can compare the contracts to make sure they are comparable. They are simple enough; you can do this yourself without additional advice. Just look at the Insurance Product Information Documents (IPIDs) and make sure the product provides the cover you want. Check the limits of cover to ensure it's enough.

If you are dealing with a high street broker, or if you have complicated requirements (e.g. ill-health, a valuable pet, or an expensive motor home) you will get good service and a decent price. There is no harm in asking for a price on the high street.

Quick Tip

It is always better to deal face to face if you can afford to do so. You know where they are if you need help. A friendly face in a time of need is always preferable to hanging on a phone trying to get through to an anonymous call centre.

ABOUT THE AUTHOR

NIGEL A ADAMS

TD VR DIP. CII STI ABIBA MLIA DIP. FCIFA

Nigel was born in the small village of Dinas Powys, just outside Cardiff, in 1964. He attended the local Church in Wales primary school and comprehensive. He was not particularly academic but loved working with his hands and gained a scholarship to the Ship Building Industry Training Board (SITB) in Southampton.

After a year completing his City and Guilds in Boatyard Joinery, he returned home to look for a full-time job. After writing over 100 applications without success, he joined his father in the family firm, Peter Adams Insurance Brokers, as a stop-gap in 1981. He continued his search for a job in joinery or boat building.

Having grown up with insurance, it wasn't long before Nigel found the industry fascinating and though he was offered a job in boat building he stayed in financial services. He found the people, the situations, the businesses, their needs, their problems and solving them, endlessly interesting. He became a director in his father's business at the age of twenty-four.

Nigel qualified with a Diploma in Insurance (Dip. CII) and was elected to the Society of Technicians in Insurance (STI), became an Associate of the British Insurance Brokers Association (ABIBA), qualified as an IFA, and became a Member of the Life Insurance Association by examination (MLIA Dip.) He was elected as an Associate and then a Fellow of the Corporation of Insurance and Financial Advisers (ACIFA, FCIFA) and served on the local South Wales British Insurance Brokers Association committee, where he was President. Nigel was appointed to the Small Business Advisory Board of the British Insurance Brokers Association in 2018.

With nearly forty years in insurance, starting as a motor clerk, Nigel has worked his way up through all the technical levels of personal and commercial insurance and was an IFA for over ten years, before deciding to concentrate on corporate risk management. After a merger he became Director of Insurance Service for the NG Insurance Group and, when that was sold in 2008, he took up a position with HIGOS, on their senior management board.

In November 2010 Nigel was itching to build something new and started Severn Bay Corporate Solutions with his wife Karen, in Cardiff. Its mission is to deliver "A first-class risk management and insurance service that exceeds expectations and delivers real value over the long term." The model is 100% fee-based, so it avoids commission-related conflicts. It covers all forms of commercial insurance and risk management, from small package business, up to international businesses with turnovers of £100m+. That mission and Nigel's passion continue to this day.

In 1984 Nigel joined the Royal Regiment of Wales (RRW) as a reserve soldier. He was commissioned at RMAS Sandhurst in 1993. He retired from the Royal Welsh in 2014 when he was a Brigade Staff Officer. He served in all major European NATO ally countries and across the world. During those thirty years he was awarded the Territorial Decoration (TD) and the Volunteer Reserve Service Medal (VRSM).

TESTIMONIALS

"When I was looking for business insurance, Nigel and his team at Severn Bay provided great customer service. Nigel is extremely knowledgeable and was thorough in his search to find an insurance to meet our requirement. Everything was clear and transparent. Nigel would always be my first port of call."

Gareth Davies
FCA Qualified Accountant

"We have used Nigel for all our business policies for the last 6 years. His industry knowledge is second to none, as is his dedication and commitment to his clients to ensure they have the right cover and best service possible."

Gary Bagstaff
Director – Print Sauce Associates

"I have known Nigel for some years and he has been in charge of our Insurances for most of that time. Nigel always gives me the pragmatic and realistic view of any questions raised and I am sure would do so in the case of any claims. Of course I have also happily recommended his firm to others for Insurance."

Bob Sheppard
Bob Sheppard Associates

"Nigel is one of those increasingly rare individuals who builds his business through developing and nurturing deep, long-term relationships and focussing as much on the Personal as the commercial aspects. Innovative in his approach to business and financial models, I have no hesitation recommending him as a personable and proactive broker with a deep knowledge and understanding of the insurance market."

Nick Pester
Partner, Head of Insurance and InsurTech
at Capital Law Ltd

"Nigel has been Global Foods' insurance broker for over 35 years. In that time the business has grown to be a national distribution company. At every stage of our development Nigel's advice and the service has been first class. When we have needed to make claims, he has always been there to help us. At every stage the service has been personal, friendly and professional. I have no hesitation in recommending Nigel."

Mr M Yaqub
Director at Global Foods Limited

"Very knowledgeable, very proactive, understands our business inside out, quick to react to issues and has delivered significant cost savings. Highly recommended."

Mike Rees
Group Financial Director, BVG Group Ltd

"I have been a client of Severn Bay Insurance for a number of years and have always found Nigel and his team to be very helpful and personable. We have, at times, required some immediate and specialist cover and they have always come through to offer us the support I need to grow my business."

Phil Grunewald
AVA Fire & Security

"I have known Nigel and his family for a couple of decades. He is a true gentleman and has the habit of gaining and retaining very happy and long-term clients!"

Jonathan Poyner
Director – Operations and Buildings at Barbican Centre and Guildhall School of Music and Drama

Lightning Source UK Ltd.
Milton Keynes UK
UKHW012307271021
392934UK00003B/65

9 781789 421019